SMOKE SCREEN

Psychological Disorders Related to Nicotine Use

THE ENCYCLOPEDIA OF PSYCHOLOGICAL DISORDERS

THE ENCYCLOPEDIA OF PSYCHOLOGICAL DISORDERS

Senior Consulting Editor Carol C. Nadelson, M.D.
Consulting Editor Claire E. Reinburg

SMOKE SCREEN

Psychological Disorders Related to Nicotine Use

Daniel Partner

CHELSEA HOUSE PUBLISHERS
Philadelphia

The ENCYCLOPEDIA OF PSYCHOLOGICAL DISORDERS provides up-to-date information on the history of, causes and effects of, and treatment and therapies for problems affecting the human mind. The titles in this series are not intended to take the place of the professional advice of a psychiatrist or mental health care professional.

Chelsea House Publishers
Editor in Chief: Stephen Reginald
Managing Editor: James D. Gallagher
Production Manager: Pamela Loos
Art Director: Sara Davis
Director of Photography: Judy L. Hasday
Senior Production Editor: LeeAnne Gelletly

Staff for SMOKE SCREEN
Prepared by P. M. Gordon Associates, Philadelphia
Picture Researcher: Susan G. Holtz
Associate Art Director: Takeshi Takahashi
Cover Designer: Brian Wible

The Chelsea House World Wide Website address is
http://www.chelseahouse.com

First Printing

9 8 7 6 5 4 3 2 1

Library of Congress Cataloging-in-Publication Data

Partner, Daniel.

    Smoke screen : psychological disorders related to nictoine use / by Daniel Partner.
       p. cm. — (Encyclopedia of psychological disorders)
    Includes bibliographical references and index.
    Summary: Describes the history and addictive nature of nicotine use in various forms and its harmful effects, with an emphasis on related psychological disorders.
    ISBN 0-7910-4958-2 (hbk.)
    1. Tobacco habit—Juvenile literature. 2. Nicotine—Juvenile literature.
    [1. Smoking. 2. Tobacco habit.] I. Title. II. Series.
    RC567.P37 1999
    616.86'5—dc21

                                  99-13338
                                    CIP

CONTENTS

PSYCHOLOGICAL DISORDERS AND THEIR EFFECT

CAROL C. NADELSON, M.D.
PRESIDENT AND CHIEF EXECUTIVE OFFICER,
The American Psychiatric Press

There are a wide range of problems that are considered psychological disorders, including mental and emotional disorders, problems related to alcohol and drug abuse, and some diseases that cause both emotional and physical symptoms. Psychological disorders often begin in early childhood, but during adolescence we see a sharp increase in the number of people affected by these disorders. It has been estimated that about 20 percent of the U.S. population will have some form of mental disorder sometime during their lifetime. Some psychological disorders appear following severe stress or trauma. Others appear to occur more often in some families and may have a genetic or inherited component. Still other disorders do not seem to be connected to any cause we can yet identify. There has been a great deal of attention paid to learning about the causes and treatments of these disorders, and exciting new research has taught us a great deal in the past few decades.

The fact that many new and successful treatments are available makes it especially important that we reject old prejudices and outmoded ideas that consider mental disorders to be untreatable. If psychological problems are identified early, it is possible to prevent serious consequences. We should not keep these problems hidden or feel shame that we or a member of our family has a mental disorder. Some people believe that something they said or did caused a mental disorder. Some people think that these disorders are "only in your head" so that you could "snap out of it" if you made the effort. This type of thinking implies that a treatment is a matter of willpower or motivation. It is a terrible burden for someone who is suffering to be blamed for his or her misery, and often people with psychological disorders are not treated compassionately. We hope that the information in this book will teach you about various mental illnesses.

The problems covered in the volumes of the ENCYCLOPEDIA OF PSYCHOLOGICAL DISORDERS were selected because they are of particular importance to young adults, because they affect them directly or because they affect family and friends. There are individual volumes on reading disorders, attention deficit and disruptive behavior disorders, and dementia—all of these are related to our abilities to learn and integrate information from the world around us. There are books on drug abuse that provide useful information about the effects of these drugs and treatments that are available for those individuals who have drug problems. Some of the books concentrate on one of the most common mental disorders, depression. Others deal with eating disorders, which are dangerous illnesses that affect a large number of young adults, especially women.

Most of the public attention paid to these disorders arises from a particular incident involving a celebrity that awakens us to our own vulnerability to psychological problems. These incidents of celebrities or public figures revealing their own psychological problems can also enable us to think about what we can do to prevent and treat these types of problems.

Most adults who smoke begin as teenagers, and every day in the United States approximately 3,000 teens take up the habit. This young smoker is 16 years old.

NICOTINE USE: AN OVERVIEW

I n the next 24 hours, approximately 3,000 Americans under the age of 18 will become regular smokers. A majority of them will continue smoking into adulthood, despite knowing the hazards they face from using tobacco and the substantial expense they will incur. Why would anyone knowingly pay so much money to do so much damage to him- or herself?

Much of the answer lies with a poisonous substance known as nicotine. Nicotine is highly addictive. The use of tobacco, which conveys nicotine into the body, is one of the most widespread forms of substance abuse. All forms of tobacco use—cigarettes, chewing tobacco, snuff, pipes, and cigars—are habit-forming; they cause dependence and, if their use is stopped, withdrawal.

People tend to use tobacco for the same reason they use many other things: it can provide a strong sensation of pleasure. But unlike most things we enjoy, tobacco contains a powerfully addictive drug. Nicotine reinforces and strengthens the desire to smoke because it affects the brain and gives the user a sense of well-being. Therefore, it is safe to say that most people use tobacco products because their bodies are dependent on nicotine. They are addicts.

How can smokers know they are addicted? They experience various sorts of severe physical and mental discomfort if they stop smoking. This is called withdrawal. After a year or two of smoking, most people continue to smoke to prevent the suffering of withdrawal. Another indicator of addiction is that the user experiences cravings for tobacco long after withdrawal symptoms pass.

In 1964 the surgeon general of the United States declared that cigarette smoking is the single most important source of preventable and premature death in the country. It is estimated that more than 400,000

Americans die each year as a result of cigarette smoking. Some 170,000 Americans die each year from smoking-related coronary heart disease. Cancers of the lung, larynx, esophagus, bladder, pancreas, and kidney also strike smokers at increased rates. Some 30 percent of cancer deaths (130,000 per year) are linked to smoking. Chronic obstructive lung diseases such as emphysema and chronic bronchitis are 10 times more likely to occur among smokers than among nonsmokers. In 1993 the United States spent approximately 50 billion dollars on health care related to tobacco. The human and financial toll on the world's population is even more staggering.

Facts such as these are a familiar litany in modern life. Yet no law, tax, or tyrant has been able to rid society of the use of tobacco. Why?

The pleasure of smoking and the addictiveness of nicotine are part of the answer, but by themselves they cannot account for the phenomenon. They particularly do not explain why every day so many people, especially teenagers, feel compelled to light their *first* cigarette. Nor do we have any social rituals that force people to smoke. At one time, in some cultures, tobacco was used for medicinal and ceremonial purposes, and people became addicted without knowing the harm they were doing to their health. Today, however, the health risks are well known, and few people believe any longer that tobacco is a medicine.

It comes down to the psychological and social aspects of smoking. People believe that smoking says something about them—about their attitude toward life and toward society. It contributes to the way they want to see themselves and the way they want others to see them.

The use of tobacco in its many forms has an aura about it—that is, marketers have created certain seductive images that draw us to its use. Smoking is presented as an act of independence, as making the smoker "cool," sophisticated, rebellious, and grown-up, as well as being pleasurable. Tobacco marketing has long targeted adolescents with these messages, because teens are often concerned about their image and want to be treated like adults. Moreover, tobacco companies know that if they do not succeed in getting someone to start smoking as a teenager, the chances are good that he or she will never start smoking.

The simple truth is that 80 percent of adult smokers became addicted by the age of 18. One study of students who use cigarettes daily found that 44 percent of them believed that they would not be smoking in five years; five to six years later, however, 73 percent of these same women and men remained daily smokers. In a 1992 survey, about 67 percent of adolescent smokers reported that they wanted to quit smoking; 70 percent said that if they could face the decision again, they would choose not to begin smoking.

Once you start, it is hard to quit. That is the nature of an addiction. Even after the pleasure has worn off, and the seeming thrill of doing something dangerous and forbidden has passed, the smoker is left with a dependence on nicotine that grows stronger every day. It is critical that individuals understand the full implications of taking that first puff.

Nicotiana tabacum—*the tobacco plant—has been grown commercially since the early 17th century. Despite efforts of government and public interest groups to deter smoking, tobacco remains a hugely profitable crop.*

1

THE USES OF
° TOBACCO

The great American writer and humorist Mark Twain loved to smoke. He claimed to have started smoking in public when he was 11 years old. The only limitation he put on his smoking was summed up in this comment: "I have made it a rule never to smoke more than one cigar at a time." Tobacco products are associated with many popular figures from recent history. It is difficult for us to think of President Franklin Delano Roosevelt without also thinking of the fancy cigarette holder he so often used, or of Prime Minister Winston Churchill without his cigars, or of the scientist Albert Einstein without his pipe. A number of current entertainers, such as Arnold Schwarzenegger, Sean Penn, Johnny Depp, Courtney Love, and Christina Ricci, seem to be cultivating similar images.

In much of our culture, through much of our modern history, cigarettes have been equated with being "hip" and independent, cigars with being sophisticated, and pipes with being intellectual. Generations of baseball players have been associated with chewing tobacco. The problem with all of these images is that they do not tell the whole truth. The truth is that tobacco use is driven by a powerful addiction to the drug nicotine, and that it is directly linked to a wide range of health problems, including cancer, heart disease, and emphysema.

TOBACCO—A HISTORY

The story of the addiction to nicotine is the same as the story of tobacco, and both go hand in hand with the European discovery of the New World. When Europeans encountered Native Americans, they discovered tobacco as well. Eventually, Europeans conquered the Native American peoples and drove them from their ancestral lands. But tobacco stayed on, exacting a huge toll among the conquerors and their descendants. For that reason, tobacco has been called the Native Americans' revenge.

The humorist Mark Twain is one of many important cultural figures who popularized tobacco use.

The tobacco plant is of the genus *Nicotiana*. The most popular and widely cultivated species today is *Nicotiana tabacum*, which is related to the potato, tomato, eggplant, chili pepper, and nightshade plants, all members of the *Solanaceae* family. Tobacco originated in Central America and is native in its original state only to the Americas.

By the time Europeans first made contact with the New World, Native Americans had been using tobacco for centuries in many ways, including religious, social, and medicinal practices. There is evidence that the plant was domesticated as early as 3500 B.C., and perhaps even earlier. The peoples of the New World believed tobacco to be a cure-all, using it as wound dressing and as a pain killer, among other things. Many Native Americans cultivated the plant extensively and considered it an important trade item. Tobacco flourished throughout North and South America, in rain forests as well as deserts, and it was smoked, chewed, eaten, sniffed, and drunk in a wide variety of forms. Bearberry leaves were often mixed with tobacco. The plants were burned together in medicine bundles, their ascending smoke carrying prayers to the Great Spirit.

In October 1492, Christopher Columbus landed in what is now the West Indies. The people there offered him dried tobacco leaves, among other gifts, and he brought these leaves back to Europe, along with seeds (tobacco seed is so small that one ounce contains about 300,000 seeds). But most Europeans did not get their first taste of tobacco until the mid-16th century, when adventurers and diplomats like France's Jean Nicot—for whom nicotine is named—began to popularize its use. Tobacco was introduced in France in 1556, Portugal in 1558, and

Europeans were introduced to the uses of tobacco when they arrived in the New World. For centuries before the arrival of Columbus, Native Americans smoked tobacco in solemn rituals and friendly, informal gatherings.

England in 1585. Around 1586, Sir Walter Raleigh is believed to have popularized pipe smoking among members of the English court.

In 1588 the colonist Thomas Harriet, along with others, began to promote smoking as a benefit to health. Apparently Harriet liked to exhale the smoke through his nose; cancer that developed there caused his death. Nevertheless, the use of tobacco spread quickly throughout Europe and much of the rest of the world.

Europeans who encountered Native Americans at the end of the 15th century found smoking to be intertwined with fellowship, ceremony, and conversation. Native Americans smoked not only for ceremonial purposes but also for relaxation. Colonial-era smokers adopted the Indian pipe—a long-stemmed pipe with a small bowl often made of clay. Because these pipes were highly breakable, they were hard to carry around and eventually people started storing them on racks at inns and coffee houses.

The Englishman John Rolfe, husband of Pocahontas, cultivated the first successful commercial tobacco crop in Virginia in 1612. Through trial and error, he produced a new variety of tobacco that was suitable for commerce and selling overseas. Within seven years tobacco had become the colony's largest export.

The negative health effects of tobacco were not initially known. In fact, European physicians of the 16th and 17th centuries subscribed to

By the time of the American Revolution, the sale of tobacco was big business. Among tobacco's many export destinations was the west coast of Africa, where well into the 19th century it was traded for slaves.

the Native American view that tobacco was an effective medicine. In 1569 a Spanish doctor named Nicolás Monardes wrote a popular history of medicinal plants of the New World, in which he claimed that tobacco could cure at least 36 health problems.

EARLY REGULATION

Despite belief in tobacco's medicinal properties, opposition to its use quickly appeared. As tobacco's popularity grew in Europe, China, Japan, and some Muslim countries, authorities tried to regulate or prohibit it. Some imposed harsh penalties for tobacco use, ranging from slitting the lips and nostrils of the offender to execution. One Chinese emperor had tobacco importers beheaded.

In 1604 King James I of England condemned smoking the "Sotweed" as "hateful" and "dangerous to the lungs." He sought to discourage the habit by raising the tax on imported tobacco by 4,000 percent. But tobacco smuggling then became a booming business, and the use and availability of the plant increased.

In 1632, 12 years after the arrival of the Mayflower, smoking in public was declared illegal in the Massachusetts Bay Colony. A similar ban was announced in New Amsterdam (the city that became New York) in 1639, and Connecticut followed suit in 1647. These early prohibitions in the New England colonies, like those in most other lands, were motivated by religious and moral beliefs rather than by health concerns.

The Roman Catholic Church did not ban tobacco as such, but it threatened to excommunicate anyone who smoked in church. Some of the clergy got around this by using snuff (a powdered form of the leaf inhaled into the nostrils), and by the end of the 17th century this practice was common in the courts of Europe.

RISE OF TOBACCO IN THE AMERICAN COLONIES

During the American colonial period, tobacco was grown mainly for pipe smoking, chewing, and snuff. Its rapid rise as a cash crop boosted the American economy and helped fuel the demand for slave labor.

In the early 18th century, a new use for tobacco arose in the tobacco-growing colonies of Maryland, Virginia, and North Carolina. Largely because of a shortage of money, people in these colonies relied on the plant as legal tender. Because many people tried to pay their debts using tobacco leaves of inferior grades, inspection laws were passed. And because of the difficulty of transferring large quantities of tobacco to cover big expenses, Virginia in 1727 adopted a system of "tobacco notes"—certificates that could be exchanged for tobacco.

By the eve of the American Revolution, the colonies were exporting more than 100 million pounds of tobacco to England every year. During the Revolutionary War, in fact, tobacco helped finance the American cause by serving as collateral for French loans to Americans.

THE 19TH CENTURY

The pure form of nicotine was isolated in 1826. Soon after, German scientists concluded that nicotine was a poison. New Englander Samuel Green agreed. In 1836 Green wrote that tobacco was useful as an insecticide but could also kill humans. Yet such warnings did little to slow the growth of the American tobacco industry in the 19th century.

For the first half of the century, Americans continued to use tobacco primarily for chewing and for smoking in pipes. But the Mexican War of 1846–48 gave the industry a new focus. Soldiers came back from Mexico and the Southwest with an affection for *cigarros* and *cigarrillos*—large and small cigars. Along with domestic cigars, these products dominated the U.S. tobacco market for the rest of the century, although chewing tobacco remained popular in the southern states.

Within two decades, cigarettes also took hold in the American market. The name *cigarette* comes from the French word meaning "small cigar," which in turn comes from the Spanish *cigarro*. Mayans and other Native Americans had smoked a primitive cigarette, but use of the modern cigarette began in Spain and other Mediterranean countries in the early 1800s. During the Crimean War of 1853–56, many British troops learned about cigarettes from their Turkish allies. (The original rolling papers were just about any kind of paper available, including, it is said, the paper tubes that were meant to be filled with gunpowder and used as cannon fuses.) By 1854, Philip Morris, an English tobacco merchant, had begun selling his own brand of cigarettes in London.

During the American Civil War (1861–65), troops of both the North and the South received tobacco with their rations. By then, American farmers had begun to cultivate "bright tobacco," which had a mild yellow leaf. These developments helped spread the use of cigarettes in the United States, as did an invention patented in 1880 by James A. Bonsack. Originally, cigarettes had to be rolled by the smoker or made one at a time in factories. Bonsack's device dropped tobacco onto a long strip of paper, rolled and pasted it, then cut individual cigarettes. Availability of

Tobacco companies have long recognized the power of advertising. Harris, Beebe, and Company attempted to cash in on the prosperity that followed the Civil War by linking its product to images of the good life. Eighty years later, in the prosperity that followed World War II, the Liggett Group tried to attract smokers with the endorsement of a well-known actor.

premade cigarettes increased the popularity of the product on both sides of the Atlantic.

At the turn of the 20th century, though still trailing cigars in popularity, cigarettes were closing the gap. By then, too, many of the companies that would become industry giants had been founded:

- In 1760 Pierre Lorillard had established a tobacco company in New York City. Today Lorillard is a division of the Loews

Corporation, with its main factory in Greensboro, North Carolina.

- J. E. Liggett and Brother was founded in St. Louis in 1849. Today, as the Liggett Group, it continues to sell tobacco products along with alcohol, pet food, and many other items.
- In 1875 the R. J. Reynolds Tobacco Company (eventually a part of RJR/Nabisco) was established to produce chewing tobacco, popular among American cowboys. The young firm used the scraps left over from the chewing tobacco to make cigarettes.
- The American Tobacco Company, founded in 1889, grew to a virtual monopoly, was broken apart in 1911, then regained its place as the industry leader by 1940; it eventually changed its name to American Brands and then split off the tobacco business as Gallaher Limited.
- In 1902 England's Philip Morris Company established a corporation in New York to market its product line, including cigarettes. Today Philip Morris is part of a conglomerate that includes General Foods and Kraft, among other companies.

THE TWENTIETH CENTURY

As the popularity of smoking increased in the early decades of the twentieth century, an antitobacco campaign appeared, and some states even banned the sale of cigarettes. But the demand for tobacco continued to rise, and new brands appealed to the public. In 1913, for example, R. J. Reynolds introduced Camel cigarettes, which a decade later accounted for 45 percent of the U.S. cigarette market.

The use of tobacco exploded during World War I (1914–18), when cigarettes were called the "soldier's smoke." U.S. troops found cigarettes an easy, quick way to smoke compared to cigars or pipes. The American commander in Europe, General John J. Pershing, went so far as to say: "You ask me what we need to win this war. I answer tobacco as much as bullets." The soldiers brought their affection for the cigarette home with them, and by 1921 this form of smoking had become the main way in which tobacco was consumed in the United States.

In the Roaring Twenties a new market opened for the tobacco industry—smoking became acceptable among women. What started out as a display of female independence soon became commonplace. In the first edition of her *Etiquette*, published in 1922, Emily Post wrote that women should feel no qualms about smoking. Soon America was in the heyday of its romance with the cigarette, as film stars and other celebrities made smoking part of their mystique.

In 1924 Philip Morris began to market Marlboro to women with the slogan "Mild as May." The American Tobacco Company, maker of the Lucky Strike brand, also targeted women with ads featuring female movie stars. Smoking rates among girls and young women tripled between 1925 and 1935.

By the end of the Roaring Twenties, all the states that had banned cigarette sales had reversed their legislation. The use of cigarettes was now too widespread to outlaw. During World War II (1939–45), cigarette sales reached an all-time high. Packs of cigarettes were included in soldiers' field rations, and tobacco companies sent millions of cigarettes to servicemen at no cost. When the soldiers came home, the companies had a massive number of loyal customers. Following the war, nearly 75 percent of American men and about 35 percent of American women smoked cigarettes regularly.

RISING HEALTH CONCERNS

As cigarettes grew more popular, articles addressing the health effects of smoking began to appear in scientific and medical journals. In 1930 researchers in Cologne, Germany, demonstrated a statistical correlation between cancer and smoking. Eight years later Dr. Raymond Pearl of Johns Hopkins University reported that smokers do not live as long as nonsmokers. By 1944 the American Cancer Society was warning about the possible harm associated with smoking.

During the 1950s, more and more evidence surfaced that linked smoking to lung cancer. Although the tobacco industry denied any such health hazard, the companies developed and promoted new products that were supposedly safer than the original cigarettes. These innovations included cigarettes with filter tips and low tar content.

At this point, when cigarette smoking had reached the height of popularity, concerns about its health dangers had also risen to a new high. Solid scientific proof linking tobacco use with specific health problems was beginning to appear. People began to understand that smoking increased the likelihood of developing cancer and other serious medical conditions, but smokers also learned that it was not easy to give up cigarettes. Little by little, users came to understand that they suffered from an addiction.

The dried-out, brown lung of a smoker (right) contrasts dramatically with the smooth, healthy lung of a nonsmoker (left) and displays what tobacco use does to the human body.

2

THE HEALTH EFFECTS OF TOBACCO USE

B y 1950 scientists and medical researchers had concluded that smokers were more likely than nonsmokers to develop cancer. But investigators had been unable to find out how tobacco use actually caused the disease. More important, though, the general public knew very little about the growing body of statistics. In 1952, however, *Reader's Digest,* a popular and influential magazine read by millions of Americans, published "Cancer by the Carton," an article detailing the dangers of smoking. The article had an enormous effect. Similar reports appeared in other periodicals. The smoking public took notice, and in the following year cigarette sales declined for the first time in more than two decades.

In 1953 Dr. Ernst L. Wynders used laboratory mice to demonstrate that the tar in cigarettes causes cancerous tumors. This kind of study, pinpointing specific ingredients, helped the tobacco industry determine how to respond. In 1954 the tobacco companies formed the Tobacco Industry Research Council (TIRC) to respond to the growing health concerns. The TIRC soon suggested that the industry offer filtered cigarettes and low-tar formulations to provide a so-called healthier smoke. Already, in 1952, P. Lorillard had marketed its Kent brand with a "micronite" filter. (Unfortunately, the filter itself contained another cancer-causing ingredient, asbestos, which was replaced a few years later.) In 1954 R. J. Reynolds followed Lorillard's lead by launching the filtered Winston brand, and in 1956 Reynolds introduced Salem, the first menthol-flavored cigarette with a filter tip. The marketing strategy paid off, and tobacco sales were soon booming again.

Meanwhile political pressure was growing in response to the increasing body of scientific evidence suggesting that smoking caused cancer. Most of these investigations had been carried out by health organizations and private researchers. The various bodies of the federal government had very little to say. In 1961 several major health organizations, including the American

WHAT HAPPENS WHEN YOU SMOKE A CIGARETTE?

More than 700 chemical additives are found in cigarettes. Some of them are classified as toxic and are not allowed in food. Once lit, a cigarette reaches a temperature of nearly 2,000 degrees Fahrenheit. This high heat helps release thousands of chemical compounds, including poisons like carbon monoxide and hydrogen cyanide, at least 43 carcinogens (substances that cause or promote cancer), and numerous mutagens (agents that can cause mutations in cells). All of these are drawn into the body when a smoker inhales.

Nicotine is found naturally in tobacco. It has no odor and no color. It is, however, both physically and psychologically addictive, and it causes those who use it to want to smoke one cigarette after another. Nicotine enters the body as tiny droplets resting on particles of tar in cigarette smoke. Inhaled into the lungs, the drug passes quickly into the bloodstream, reaching the brain within about 10 seconds. In another 5 to 10 seconds the nicotine has spread to all parts of the body.

The nicotine raises both the heart rate and blood pressure. The smoker quickly feels more alert and relaxed. In less than 30 minutes, however, about half of the nicotine has left the bloodstream, and the smoker starts feeling less alert, more edgy. So he or she reaches for another cigarette to get a new "hit" of nicotine. Over time, the smoker starts needing more cigarettes throughout the day to satisfy the craving.

There are other results as well. The tar from tobacco smoke starts to accumulate on the bronchial tubes leading to the lungs. The hot smoke burns the tiny hairlike projections (called cilia) that trap harmful particles before they enter the lungs.

Smoking also increases the level of carbon monoxide in the lungs. This poisonous gas is quickly absorbed into the blood, reducing its capacity to carry oxygen. As a result, the smoker has to exert more physical effort to achieve a given task than does a nonsmoker. The heart in particular must work harder, especially during rigorous exercise. Increased levels of carbon monoxide in the blood can impair vision, perception of time, and coordination.

Over the years a smoker will be more likely to develop respiratory ailments, thickening of the arteries, blood clots (which can lead to heart attacks and strokes), cancer (of the lung, cervix, larynx, mouth, esophagus, bladder, pancreas, and kidney), and emphysema, as well as exhibit symptoms such as reduced stamina, poor athletic performance, wheezing, coughing, dizziness, and nausea. In time, a smoker suffers increased resistance to the flow of air into the lungs and reduced lung capacity. Besides these serious problems, prolonged tobacco use leads to stained teeth and fingers and bad breath. Even a smoker's clothes and living quarters tend to smell of tobacco.

The pleasurable effects of nicotine are only temporary. In a short while, the feeling of relaxation, well-being, and alertness begins to fade, and the smoker has to consume more and more cigarettes to maintain this feeling.

The stain on this filter is tar, one of the ingredients in cigarettes that causes cancer. In an unsuccessful effort to produce a safe product, the tobacco industry introduced the filter-tipped cigarette in the 1950s.

Cancer Society and the American Heart Association, urged President John F. Kennedy to take action regarding tobacco use and its risks. The president responded by creating the Surgeon General's Advisory Committee on Smoking and Health. Three years later the committee's 387-page report, *Smoking and Health*, stated unequivocally that "cigarette smoking is causally related to lung cancer in men." It said that the data for women, "though less extensive, point in the same direction." The report noted that the average smoker is nine to ten times more likely than the average nonsmoker to develop lung cancer and cited specific carcinogens in cigarette smoke, including cadmium, DDT, and arsenic. *Smoking and Health* also pointed to a relationship between smoking and heart disease and claimed that overall tobacco use contributed to hundreds of thousands of deaths each year.

The impact of the surgeon general's report was enormous. Sales of cigarettes dropped almost immediately by nearly 20 percent. (The decline did not last, however, as sales reached a new high the following year.) In 1965 Congress passed the Federal Cigarette Labeling and Advertising Act, which required that each pack of cigarettes carry the following warning: "Caution: Cigarette smoking may be hazardous to your health." The same year cigarette ads were taken off British television. In 1968 Bravo, a nontobacco cigarette brand made primarily of lettuce, came on the market. It failed miserably, but political pressure on the industry continued to heat up. In 1971 advertisements for tobacco products were banned from U.S. television and radio, and ads appearing in newspapers and magazines and on billboards were required to print the same warning that appeared on packs of cigarettes.

The negative press about tobacco had other effects. The major companies began to diversify their products and alter their identities. Philip Morris bought the Miller Brewing Company, maker of Miller beers. R. J. Reynolds dropped the word "tobacco" from its name to become R. J. Reynolds Industries, and it began to invest in other products, such as aluminum. The American Tobacco Company also changed its name, becoming American Brands, Inc.

In 1977 the first nationwide Great American Smokeout promoted abstinence from smoking. Three years later, the surgeon general issued another report, *The Health Consequences of Smoking for Women*. Even so, Virginia Slims cigarettes sought to profit from the growing women's rights movement with an advertising slogan that proclaimed "You've Come a Long Way Baby!" The number of female smokers began to increase, as did the number of women who developed lung cancer and other tobacco-related diseases. By 1985 lung cancer had become the leading cause of death among American women.

During the 1980s lawsuits were filed against the tobacco industry because of the harmful effects of its products, and in many areas smoking was prohibited in public places. In 1982 the surgeon general reported that "secondhand" cigarette smoke may cause lung cancer. (Secondhand or environmental smoke is the smoke that nonsmokers inhale when they are near a smoker.) Smoking in public areas was soon severely restricted, especially in the workplace. Also in 1982 Philip Morris moved into other product areas by investing in General Foods Corporation and Kraft, Inc. R. J. Reynolds also diversified by buying Nabisco and becoming RJR/Nabisco. (In 1999 its tobacco operations were sold to a Japanese company.)

In 1987 Congress banned smoking on all domestic airline flights lasting less than two hours. Three years later the ban was extended to cover all domestic flights, except those to Alaska and Hawaii. During the 1980s and 1990s the tobacco industry began to market its products

TOBACCO FACTS

- Each year, smoking kills more than 276,000 men and 142,000 women in the United States.

- One in every five deaths in the United States is tobacco related.

- About 10 million people in the United States have died from causes attributed to smoking (including heart disease and emphysema and other respiratory diseases) since the surgeon general's first report on smoking and health was published in 1964—and 2 million of these deaths were from lung cancer alone.

- From 1960 to 1990, deaths from lung cancer among women increased by more than 400 percent, exceeding breast cancer deaths for the first time in the mid-1980s.

- The American Cancer Society estimated that in 1994 alone 64,300 women died from lung cancer, whereas 44,300 died from breast cancer.

- Men who smoke increase their risk of dying from lung cancer by more than 22 times and from bronchitis and emphysema by nearly 10 times.

- Women who smoke increase their risk of dying from lung cancer by nearly 12 times and from bronchitis and emphysema by more than 10 times.

- Smoking triples the risk of dying from heart disease among middle-aged men and women.

- Every year in the United States, premature deaths from smoking rob more than five million years from the potential lifespans of smokers who have died.

- On average, smokers die nearly seven years earlier than nonsmokers.

- Annually, exposure to secondhand smoke (environmental tobacco smoke, or ETS) causes an estimated 3,000 deaths from lung cancer among American adults.

- Scientific studies also link secondhand smoke with heart disease.

In the 1980s American tobacco companies began to market cigarettes heavily overseas, particularly in Asia. Here, Buddhist monks in Cambodia collect their daily donation beneath a sign advertising the Marlboro brand.

more heavily in areas outside the United States, especially in developing countries in Asia. This strategy paid off: at a worth of more than 30 million dollars, Philip Morris's Marlboro cigarettes became the most valuable brand of any product in the world.

THE HEALTH SITUATION TODAY

Today, many health officials and others consider the use of tobacco products to be the most critical public health problem in the United States. According to the U.S. Centers for Disease Control and Prevention, the leading preventable cause of death among Americans is tobacco use. It results in more than 400,000 premature deaths and more than

MORTALITY RELATED TO CIGARETTE SMOKING

Causes of Death	Men	Women	Overall
Cancers			
Lung	81,179	35,741	116,920
Lung from environmental tobacco smoke (ETS)	1,055	1,945	3,000
Other	21,659	9,743	31,402
Total	103,893	47,429	151,322
Cardiovascular Diseases			
Hypertension	3,233	2,151	5,450
Heart disease	88,644	45,591	134,235
Stroke	14,978	8,303	23,281
Other	11,682	5,172	16,854
Total	118,603	61,117	179,820
Respiratory Diseases			
Pneumonia	11,292	7,881	19,173
Bronchitis/emphysema	9,234	5,541	14,865
Chronic airway obstruction	30,385	18,579	48,982
Other	787	668	1,455
Total	51,788	32,689	84,475
Diseases Among Infants	1,006	705	1,711
Burn Deaths	863	499	1,362
All Causes	276,153	142,537	418,690

Sources: Centers for Disease Control and Prevention, American Cancer Society, and U.S. Environmental Protection Agency.

$50 billion in direct medical costs in the United States each year. Smoking kills more U.S. citizens every year than AIDS, alcohol abuse, drug abuse, car crashes, murders, suicides, and fires combined! Furthermore, according to the U.S. surgeon general, more than 50,000 nonsmokers die annually because of their exposure to environmental, or secondhand, tobacco smoke.

Underlying this enormous medical, social, and financial burden is nicotine addiction. A highly addictive drug that occurs naturally in the tobacco plant, nicotine is the substance that gets people "hooked," although other ingredients of smoke, such as tar and dangerous gases, bring on most of the long-term health problems. Nicotine dependence is the most common substance-use disorder in the United States.

It appears that nicotine is at least as addictive as other drugs considered a social problem. For example, among persons who experiment with alcohol, 10 to 15 percent will become dependent on it at some point in their lives. Among those who experiment with cigarettes, however, nearly twice as many (20 to 30 percent) will become nicotine dependent. A majority of cigarette smokers exhibit the recognized signs of drug dependence: they have difficulty giving up the habit, they suffer withdrawal symptoms when they do stop, and they continue using the drug despite their knowledge of the personal harm it can cause.

In another area of health concern, nicotine dependence and withdrawal can make the diagnosis and treatment of psychiatric disorders difficult. For example, symptoms of nicotine withdrawal, such as restlessness and insomnia, can be confused with symptoms of other psychiatric disorders and conditions, such as alcohol withdrawal. Smoking decreases the blood levels of several medications, and nicotine withdrawal can worsen the symptoms of other psychiatric conditions in some patients.

In recent years, various medications and behavioral therapies have been developed to treat nicotine addiction. Consumers can now easily purchase effective treatments such as the nicotine patch and nicotine gum in drugstores and supermarkets. Research has shown, however, that treating addiction with medications alone is not nearly as effective as coupling them with some form of behavioral therapy.

LEGAL ACTION

The first product liability suits against the tobacco industry were brought in St. Louis in 1954 and have continued ever since. In the 1980s

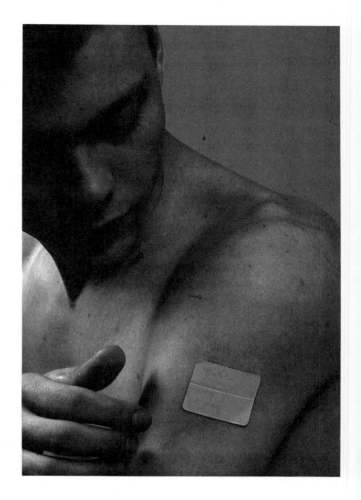

Because nicotine is an addictive drug, smokers often need to rely on medication to help wean themselves from it. The nicotine patch delivers controlled doses of nicotine through the skin, thus alleviating the craving for tobacco.

and 1990s the litigation began to rely on new legal theories regarding liability and the withholding of safety warnings. Yet only a handful of suits by individuals and families succeeded in convincing U.S. juries to award monetary damages.

In 1994 the attorneys general of Mississippi and West Virginia took the matter into their own hands. They filed suits against the tobacco industry on behalf of their state governments. Soon more and more states took similar steps. The various states had spent billions, under Medicaid and other programs, to treat illnesses caused by tobacco, and officials sought to recover some of those expenses. The states also argued that they had been wronged by acts of the tobacco industry in violation of antitrust, consumer protection, and other laws.

On November 23, 1998, after much heated discussion and political maneuvering, 46 states plus the District of Columbia and four U.S. territories agreed on a settlement with five American tobacco companies. The plaintiffs agreed to drop their lawsuits against the tobacco industry in exchange for payments of more than $200 billion, beginning in 2001 and continuing through the year 2025, with more than $32 billion of that amount coming in the first five years. (The four other states—Mississippi, Florida, Texas, and Minnesota—had reached their own settlements earlier. The total payments from the tobacco industry to all 50 states should reach $246 billion dollars.)

It is expected that most states will use at least some of the money to help fund new programs to help smokers quit and to discourage non-smokers from starting. States that have many tobacco farmers, such as North Carolina and Kentucky, may use some of the settlement money to provide assistance to farmers. Many antismoking experts argue that if states do not allocate a substantial amount of their awards to prevention efforts, in the long run settlement may not result in fewer smokers.

Many experts also believe that much, if not most, of the cost of the settlement will ultimately be paid by smokers themselves—through substantially increased prices for tobacco products.

SMOKELESS TOBACCO IS STILL HARMFUL

Many people seem to think that chewing tobacco and snuff are safe substitutes for cigarettes. But the truth is that they are not safe. Such unburned tobacco products contain carcinogens that have caused malignant tumors in animals. The Third National Cancer Survey found that men who used smokeless tobacco had a nearly fourfold increased risk of developing oral cancer compared with nonusers. Women who reported long-term use had approximately a 50-fold increased risk of developing cancer of the gums. Such cancers are found throughout the oral cavity. Benign oral tumors can occur after only a few years of smokeless tobacco use. With smokers, cancer is most likely to develop in the lungs, although smoking can also lead to cancer within the oral cavity.

The use of smokeless tobacco causes other problems. Gums may recede from teeth in the spot where tobacco is held in the mouth. This

SMOKELESS TOBACCO AND BASEBALL

Chewing tobacco was the most popular form of tobacco in 1847, the year the rules of baseball were adopted. But in the 1880s, when scientists discovered that bacteria caused tuberculosis, people realized that spitting spread the disease. Because tuberculosis was the leading cause of death at the turn of the century, tobacco chewing declined and men switched to cigarettes. But in the ballpark smokeless tobacco seemed to have season tickets. Some players said they used it to keep their mouths from getting dry in the heat and dust of a nine-inning ballgame; others claimed that chewing tobacco enhanced their reaction time by keeping them alert.

But peer pressure may have been the real reason ballplayers continued to chew tobacco. When the former Dodger Rex Barney was an 18-year-old rookie pitcher in the minor leagues, one day in the bullpen his coach told him, "You'll never get to the major leagues unless you chew tobacco."

In the 1950s, when baseball games first went on television, cigarette companies were among the main sponsors. Fans smoked the brand that sponsored their favorite team. The players did too: the Giants were sponsored by Chesterfield, and that was the players' brand. For a time, it seemed smoking might replace chewing as the ballplayers' habit of choice.

By the 1970s the dangers of smoking were well known, so players went back to chewing tobacco because they thought it was safer than cigarettes. Then snuff dipping entered the scene for the first time, aided by the delivery of free samples to team clubhouses. Tobacco companies recruited players to appear in ads for snuff; and the use of moist snuff subsequently increased 15-fold among boys aged 17 to 19.

In 1987 warning labels went on the cans and pouches of smokeless tobacco. In 1988 teams banned free samples from their clubhouses. In 1990 Major League Baseball issued a report on the hazards of smokeless tobacco and announced new efforts to help players beat the habit.

causes tooth loss. And increased tooth decay can result from the large amount of sugar contained in chewing tobacco.

Studies show that the elevated levels of nicotine in the blood that result from using smokeless tobacco are similar to those produced by smoking cigarettes. Persons who use snuff or chewing tobacco experience increases in heart rate and blood pressure similar to those experienced by smokers. And the use of smokeless tobacco is linked with head and neck cancer.

Smokeless tobacco is just as addictive as smoking tobacco, and regular use is likely to result in long-term nicotine dependence and its associated health risks. Snuff and chewing tobacco also quickly diminish the senses of taste and smell, and these drugs increase bad breath.

■　　　　　■　　　　　■

The actor Yul Brynner died of cancer in 1985 at the age of 70. Brynner, who was very successful in Hollywood, is best known for his role as the King of Siam in the movie *The King and I*. Before he died he made a videotape for the American Cancer Society to help in its effort to combat smoking. In the tape he says, "I really wanted to make a commercial when I discovered that I was that sick, and my time was so limited. To make a commercial that says, simply, 'Now that I'm gone, I tell you, *Don't smoke*. Whatever you do, *Just don't smoke*. If I could take back that smoking, I wouldn't be talking about any cancer. I'm convinced of that.'"

Parents who smoke are gambling with their children's health. Secondhand cigarette smoke has been linked to increased incidences of asthma in children and sudden infant death syndrome (SIDS).

3

WOMEN, CHILDREN, AND NICOTINE

In many countries, tobacco use is mainly a male behavior, so nicotine addiction among women is rare. This used to be the case in the United States as well, but in recent decades it appears that the difference between the sexes may have narrowed considerably. Estimates indicate that about 78 percent of men aged 15 to 54 acknowledge that they have smoked, compared with 73 percent of women of the same ages. Of this group, 33 percent of men and 31 percent of women have developed a dependence on tobacco. It is estimated that 26 percent of the men and 23 percent of the women will develop a lifetime nicotine addiction.

The number of smokers in the United States declined in the 1970s and 1980s, and it stabilized in the 1990s. But this overall downturn was greater among men than among women. It is still the case that more men smoke than women, but the difference is slight and the incidence of smoking may soon be greater among women. Several factors have contributed to this trend. Two of the most important are the increase in the number of girls and young women who begin smoking and the fact that women are less likely than men to quit.

Why are there differences in the smoking behavior of men and women? Differences in nicotine sensitivity may be the cause. Studies indicate that women smoke fewer cigarettes per day, use brands with lower nicotine content, and do not inhale as deeply as men. It is not yet conclusively known, however, if this is because the sexes differ in their sensitivity to nicotine. Research has found that women may be more affected by factors such as the sensory aspects of smoke or social factors than they are by nicotine itself.

Smoking-cessation studies show that women are less likely to decide to quit than men and may be more likely to relapse if they do quit. In cessation programs using nicotine replacement methods, such as the patch or gum, the nicotine does not seem to reduce craving as effectively for women as it does for men. There are other factors as well. For example, the withdrawal experience

FEMALE SMOKING RATES BY RACE OR ETHNICITY (AGE 18 AND OLDER)

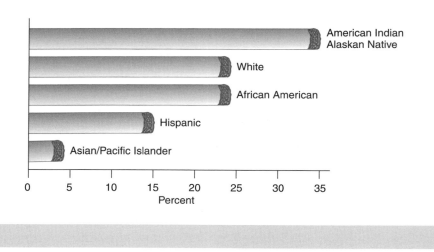

may be more intense for women, and they are more likely than men to gain weight upon quitting. So standard treatment may have to be adjusted to compensate for gender differences in nicotine sensitivity.

It is currently estimated that about 22 million (22 percent) women 18 years and older and at least 1.5 million adolescent girls in the United States smoke cigarettes. Although the prevalence of smoking among men dropped 24 percentage points from 1965 to 1993, the prevalence of smoking among women dropped only 11 percentage points during the same period. Because women continue to begin smoking at younger ages, they become dependent earlier and increase their risks of developing smoking-related diseases.

Among female high school seniors, the number of daily smokers rose from 18 percent in 1991 to 24 percent in 1997. The more formal education a woman receives, the less likely she is to smoke. In 1995, 40 percent of women between the ages of 25 and 44 who did not finish high school were smokers; 34 percent of high school graduates were smokers; 24 percent of those with some college were smokers; and only 14 percent of those who had graduated from college were smokers.

The increase in female smoking has led to a tragic rise in tobacco-

The Truth About Tobacco and Performance

"If my opponents smoke, I'm halfway to a shutout."
—U.S. Goalie

Smoking cuts down on fitness. So if you smoke, you're not going to be able to run as *fast* or as *far* as your smoke-free teammates — or opponents!

Smoking slows down lung growth and reduces lung function. That can leave you gulping for air when you need it the most!

"To shut down their offense, I've got to be quick. Cigarettes just slow you down."
—U.S. Defender

In fact, teen smokers suffer from shortness of breath almost three times as often as teens who don't smoke. Breath is something an athlete can't *afford* to be short of!

Compared to nonsmokers at rest, the hearts of young adult smokers beat an extra two or three times per minute. So in competition, your body wastes a lot of heartbeats just trying to keep up with nonsmokers!

"Show me a defender who smokes and I'll show a GOAL."
—U.S. Midfielder

Teen smokers produce phlegm (yuck!) more than twice as often as teens who don't smoke. Ever try breathing and spitting at the same time?

Three out of four teens who are daily smokers say they keep smoking because it's really hard to quit. Do you want to be hooked on nicotine or sports?

"Personally, I prefer to smoke defenders."
—U.S. Striker

Teens who smoke are more likely to drink heavily and use illegal drugs such as marijuana and cocaine. So if you think, "It's just cigarettes," think again.

The long-term health effects of smoking may seem to be in the distant future, but they're *real*. Each year, smoking kills more people than AIDS, alcohol, drug abuse, car crashes, murders, suicides, and fires — *combined!* Smoking and athletic performance definitely don't mix.

Aimed at teenagers, this poster offers basic facts about how smoking affects young adults. Tobacco use among children is a major public health issue. Parents, teachers, community leaders, and politicians all need to address this growing threat to our nation's youth.

TOBACCO ADVERTISING AND PROMOTION

According to information compiled by STAT (Stop Teenage Addiction to Tobacco), of Northeastern University in Boston:

Tobacco products are among the most heavily advertised in the United States. In 1994 alone, more than a billion dollars was spent on cigarette advertising and promotion.

Teenagers are more than twice as likely as adults to smoke the three most heavily advertised brands of cigarettes—Marlboro, Camel, and Newport (86 percent of teens, compared with 35 percent of adults).

Tobacco companies' expenditures for specialty gift items (such as T-shirts, caps, sunglasses, key chains, calendars, and sporting goods) that bear a cigarette logo rose from $340 million in 1992 to $756 million in 1993, an increase of 122 percent.

Banned from advertising on television and radio, tobacco companies have found creative ways to keep their brand names before the public, such as sponsoring NASCAR races and other sporting events.

In the 1990s, controversy surrounded the image of "Joe Camel." Child welfare advocates said the cartoon character was aimed at children, but the tobacco industry denied this. In any event, more than 90 percent of 6-year-olds knew the name "Joe Camel" and knew that he was all about smoking.

Tobacco-marketing dollars pay for promotional activities that have special appeal to young people, such as concerts, sporting events, and other public entertainment; for distributing specialty items bearing product names and logos; and for issuing coupons and premiums.

Tobacco advertising and promotion influence adolescents' decision to begin smoking more than peer pressure does.

The recent rise in adolescent smoking coincided with large-scale cigarette promotional campaigns.

Studies in the mid-1990s showed that 30 percent of 3-year-olds and 91 percent of 6-year-olds could identify "Joe Camel" as a symbol for smoking.

A 1992 Gallup survey found that one-half of youth smokers and one-quarter of youth who do not smoke owned at least one tobacco promotional item.

related health problems, many of which are unique to women. More than 152,000 women died from diseases related to smoking in 1994. From 1960 to 1990 the death rate from lung cancer among women increased by more than 400 percent, and the rate is still rising. In 1987 lung cancer surpassed breast cancer as the number one cause of cancer deaths among women. The American Cancer Society estimated that in 1998 lung cancer killed 67,000 women, compared with 43,500 women who died from breast cancer.

NICOTINE AND PREGNANCY

Smoking can damage women's reproductive health and is associated with reduced fertility and early menopause. Women who smoke during pregnancy subject themselves and their developing fetus and newborn to special risks, including pregnancy complications, premature birth, low birth weight, stillbirth, and infant death. Research suggests that the fetus of a mother who smokes and the baby exposed to secondhand smoke after delivery have an increased risk of sudden infant death syndrome (SIDS).

Another problem attributed to smoking is the growing incidence of asthma. In the United States between 8,000 and 26,000 children are diagnosed with asthma every year. The odds of developing asthma are twice as high among children whose mothers smoke at least 10 cigarettes a day. Between 400,000 and one million asthmatic children have their condition worsened by exposure to secondhand smoke. Efforts to reduce smoking among young women can save money in the long run: for every dollar invested in smoking cessation programs for pregnant women, about six dollars is saved in the cost of neonatal intensive care and long-term care associated with low-birth-weight deliveries.

When a pregnant woman inhales tobacco smoke, carbon monoxide (a lethal gas) and nicotine interfere with the amount of oxygen supplied to her fetus. The nicotine easily crosses the placental membrane, and nicotine levels in the fetal blood have been found to be 15 percent higher than in the mother's blood. Nicotine also concentrates in the amniotic fluid and breast milk. It is likely that these factors account for the delays in development that are common in the fetuses and infants of women who smoke.

Women who smoke during pregnancy are also at greater risk of delivering prematurely than are nonsmokers. For infants carried to term, there is a risk of low birth weight. It is estimated that at least 20 percent of pregnant women in the United States smoke throughout their pregnancies. The adverse effects of their smoking may occur in any trimester of pregnancy. There may be a spontaneous abortion, premature delivery, or decreased birth weight. In fact, the more a woman smokes during pregnancy, the less her infant weighs. On the other hand, those who give up smoking early in their pregnancy have infants of similar weight to those of nonsmokers.

TOBACCO USE BY CHILDREN AND TEENS

"I smoked my first cigarette when I was in second grade," recalls John, now the father of three children. "I was sitting in the woods with my best friend, Brian."

Brian's father was a cigarette salesman, and in those days—the 1950s—tobacco companies used to distribute small sample packs containing four or five cigarettes. "Well, Brian's garage was full of boxes

Smoking during pregnancy is dangerous to the unborn child. This young woman is subjecting her fetus to high doses of nicotine and carbon monoxide and putting it at risk for premature delivery and low birth weight.

CIGARS—A COMEBACK?

One of the surprising tobacco-related developments of the 1990s was the sudden reemergence of cigar smoking as a popular, and increasingly socially acceptable, activity among men and women, young and old. In a matter of only five years cigar smoking increased by 50 percent. A survey of high school students in Massachusetts found that 25 percent of boys and 6 percent of girls had smoked a cigar in the past month. A national survey found that six million high school students had smoked at least one cigar in the past year, and about 3 percent of them had become frequent cigar smokers, lighting up at least once a week.

Cigar smoking has become a noticeable fad in the United States. Entire magazines are devoted to the practice, and the product routinely shows up in the mouths of celebrities on television. The actor Arnold Schwarzenegger and the

Cigar smoking grew into a socially acceptable fad in the 1990s, with many celebrities— including the President of the United States—taking up the habit. But as a risk factor for cancer of the mouth, esophagus, and pancreas, smoking a cigar is just as dangerous as smoking a cigarette.

hockey star Wayne Gretzky have both appeared on the cover of *Cigar Aficionado* magazine. Many people, influenced by such images, mistakenly think that because athletes and other high-profile public figures are smoking cigars, they must not be as dangerous as cigarettes. A 1998 study by the National Cancer Institute found such beliefs to be completely wrong. The report stated that "cigar smoke is tobacco smoke" and pointed out that many of the 4,000 compounds it contains can cause cancer or are otherwise poisonous. The death rate from cancers of the mouth and esophagus is about the same for cigar smokers as it is for cigarette smokers. Strong evidence was found linking cigar smoking with cancer of the pancreas, a particularly deadly form of cancer.

In 1997 the Food and Drug Administration introduced new rules that were supposed to restrict young people's access to tobacco by prohibiting retailers from selling cigarettes and smokeless tobacco products to anyone under the age of 18. But the regulations did not mention cigars and pipe tobacco. The result was that teenagers who could not purchase cigarettes were allowed to buy cigars. And they did, in large numbers. Even if the FDA restrictions are extended to all forms of tobacco, it may well take many years to reverse the growing popularity of cigars, and even longer to begin to counteract the health damage that will have been done.

containing these sample packs, so we took a few of them and ran off to our treehouse in the woods. Brian had never smoked before either. We each lit up a cigarette."

John recalls that shortly after taking his first puff he started feeling sick. "I don't think I ever felt so ill, so fast. I threw up. Brian threw up. We felt just awful."

Thinking back on the experience, John says, "You'd think that we would have decided then and there that smoking was a terrible activity, one that we would never want to repeat." But that was not the case. Over the next few years he and Brian continued to smoke cigarettes in their remote treehouse. "After a while, we both started getting used to it, and then we started looking forward to it. The truth is, I was addicted to nicotine before I was 10 years old."

Why did John feel so compelled to smoke? "Cigarettes were all around. Both of my parents smoked, my aunts and uncles and grandfather smoked. It seemed like everyone on TV smoked, including musicians and athletes. It just seemed like something I had to do in order to be grown up."

John started trying to quit smoking when he was about 20, but he wasn't successful until his first child was born, a dozen years later. "I took one look at my daughter and vowed that I would never smoke again. And I didn't." Unfortunately, John's father could not stop. "He's 73 now, and he's had emphysema for over 10 years. He has to sleep in a chair, and he can't leave the house without taking his oxygen tank with him. I can't imagine a worse way to die."

John is pleased that his daughters have a very different view of smoking than he did as a youngster. "My kids have almost no relatives who smoke. They think it is one of the filthiest, smelliest, disgusting things a person can do. They just can't stand to be anywhere near tobacco smoke."

■   ■   ■

John began smoking much earlier than most smokers in the United States, where the average user starts at age 14. But his reasons for taking his first puffs are similar to those given by young teenagers today. They often light up for the first time on a dare or to prove that they are "cool" or "tough." Tobacco companies understand these attitudes very well. That is why they have long marketed their products to young people. From a business standpoint, this approach is understandable—they need to find, or create, new smokers every day to take the place of those adults who quit or die. Teenagers are particularly vulnerable to advertising campaigns that make cigarettes seem attractive and grown-up.

As a result, about a million American kids start smoking every year— a rate of approximately 3,000 new smokers every single day. Almost 10 percent of 13-year-olds smoke regularly; that figure rises to about 25 percent for all American teens. Many of them understand the health risks involved. Often they have been exposed to sophisticated antismoking campaigns in their schools and communities. They have watched movies depicting the awful things that long-term tobacco use can do to the human body. Yet they take up the habit anyway. Why?

Many teens are persuaded by friends or siblings to start. Others feel they need to smoke to be accepted socially. Some say they smoke to control their weight. Rebelliousness is another frequently cited reason given for tobacco use: because they are told so often not to smoke, many young men and women will light up out of simple defiance. A great

More than a million teenagers take up smoking every year, often for no better reason than to impress their friends. Tobacco companies need younger smokers to replace older ones who quit—or die.

number of teenagers argue that they smoke only to reduce the stresses of school and that they intend to quit soon. What they learn, though, is that regular tobacco use can quickly cease being a simple choice. Once a person's body becomes accustomed to receiving a regular dose of nicotine, it starts demanding it. Stopping becomes more and more difficult.

Tobacco advertising has long been filled with images intended to appeal to the vulnerabilities of young people. There are the tough, independent guys (Marlboro Man), the cool dudes (Joe Camel), and the glamorous models (hired by Virginia Slims). For the better part of a century, cigarette smokers have been depicted as young, attractive, popular, and successful. Every time another teenager becomes addicted to nicotine, tobacco companies can feel assured that their advertising dollars have been well spent. The industry has not bothered to inform us of the dangers of smoking. And it has not mentioned the fate of the first Marlboro Man, the model David Millar, who died of emphysema caused by his own smoking.

A worker trying to cope with stress or a boring routine may seek relief by reaching for a cigarette. Through its effect on the nervous system, nicotine can improve memory, reduce tension—and cause addiction.

4

THE CAUSES AND EFFECTS OF NICOTINE ADDICTION

L ike addiction to cocaine or opiates (which include heroin, morphine, and opium), the habitual use of tobacco is considered a substance-use disorder. Users become dependent on nicotine just as they do on "hard" drugs. That is, over time, a user grows more tolerant of the drug, often needs more of it to produce the same effect, and experiences withdrawal symptoms when the drug is denied.

But why does someone start smoking in the first place? Most people begin smoking cigarettes in their teenage years. Adolescents may be encouraged to smoke by the ads they see, peer pressure of friends and schoolmates, or the example of their parents or other family members. Tobacco use is also common among adolescents who abuse other drugs. A young person may not be adequately informed about the addictive nature of the nicotine in cigarette tobacco, and some teenagers simply do not believe they are susceptible to such addiction. Therefore, individuals may smoke for a while, attempt to quit, and then relapse into smoking again.

This pattern is similar to the process of addiction to other drugs. Indeed in many ways tobacco addiction resembles opiate addictions. This is serious, because it has been found that drug use evolves through developmental stages; that is, there is a distinct pattern of stages in a person's initiation into drug use. These stages are:

1. No use of any drugs

2. Use of beer or wine

3. Use of cigarettes

4. Use of marijuana

5. Use of heroin, cocaine, and other drugs

CURT SCHILLING'S STORY

During the 1997 baseball season, Philadelphia's pitcher Curt Schilling won 17 games with the Phillies and led the majors with 319 strikeouts. At that time he had been chewing tobacco for more than 15 years. He had often tried to kick his habit and had even become violently ill in the attempt—throwing up all night, sweating, and experiencing severe headaches.

Because so many professional baseball players chew tobacco, players can volunteer for an oral examination as part of their annual physicals. (The players' association and the players' relations committee are striving to make such exams mandatory.) At spring training before the 1998 season, Schilling had such an oral exam. Doctors found a leukoplakia (precancerous lesion) in his mouth, a result of his habit of chewing tobacco. The lesion was removed, but Schilling's doctor said there was a 100 percent chance that his condition would develop into cancer if he did not stop chewing immediately.

The 6'4", 230-pound pitcher faced a task even more difficult than pitching to major league hitters. He had to do something that he had not been able to achieve in the past. After years of chewing tobacco, he had to give up the habit. He knew it would be difficult, but he committed himself to the struggle, and since then he has often spoken out against the dangers of the habit.

Not all people who smoke cigarettes go through these stages. But it is true that those who proceed to the latter stages of drug use usually have progressed through the earlier stages step-by-step. It is not a certainty that a person who smokes cigarettes will go on to use other drugs, but it is possible. Not everyone who uses marijuana, even extensively, uses cocaine. But clinical studies show that people tend to add to the mix of drugs they use rather than substitute one drug for another. So, adolescents who start with alcoholic beverages will continue to drink, and perhaps more often and in greater amounts than before. Next they might start using nicotine-containing products such as cigarettes. And when they drink, they usually smoke more. Users of cigarettes, alcohol, and opiates also show similar patterns of abstinence and relapse.

Phillies pitching ace Curt Schilling had to give up chewing tobacco after doctors found a precancerous lesion in his mouth. But quitting was hard for Schilling; his previous attempts had ended in failure after bouts of nausea, headaches, and sweating.

Smoking is not as common in the United States as it once was. But tobacco use has declined less among those who are young, female, non-Caucasian, less educated, or poor, as well as among those with psychiatric or alcohol and drug problems. The psychiatric markers of someone with a tendency to begin smoking include the use and abuse of alcohol and other drugs, attention deficit disorders, and depressive symptoms.

Researchers have identified several classifications of cigarette smokers. *Craving* (or psychologically and physically addicted) smokers have a physical need for nicotine and go through withdrawal if they do not get it. Most smokers fit this classification, since every habitual smoker is addicted to nicotine. Beyond their addiction, however, individuals may

Researchers have found that people use tobacco for a variety of reasons. Most smokers report that they light up for the sense of pleasure or relaxation it gives them.

also smoke for one or more reasons. *Crutch* (or tension-reduction) smokers use cigarettes to manage negative circumstances, stressful situations, or feelings of anger, fear, and anxiety. The cigarette acts like a tranquilizer—it helps the person manage his or her tension. The fact is that people smoke more when they are under stress because stress reduces the level of nicotine in the body. The loss of nicotine intensifies their tension, so they combat this stress by replacing the lost nicotine. *Habitual* smokers have developed behavioral patterns that cause them to light a cigarette in response to a cue, such as pouring a cup of coffee, getting into a car, or completing a meal. *Handling* (or oral-gratification) smokers like the trappings and the ritual of smoking. These may include opening the package, tapping a cigarette, striking the match, and handling the lit cigarette. *Pleasure* (or relaxation) smokers, about two-thirds of all smokers, enjoy the feelings of contentment or satisfaction they receive when they are smoking. The effect of nicotine on the brain helps them feel good about themselves. Finally, *stimulation* smokers get a lift from smoking. The nicotine in a cigarette helps them perk up, feel more energetic and alert.

BODY, MIND, AND NICOTINE

The list of national and international organizations that recognize nicotine as an addictive substance is very long. It includes the Office of the U.S. Surgeon General, the World Health Organization, the American Medical Association, the American Psychiatric Association, the American Psychological Association, the American Society of Addiction Medicine, and the Medical Research Council in the United Kingdom.

But what is an addictive drug? Definitions vary, but they all share several key components. The first is that the drug causes compulsive use despite the knowledge of its harmful effects. Second, the drug has a direct chemical effect on the brain. Third, using the drug is accompanied by actions that encourage continued use. Finally, withdrawal symptoms occur when a user attempts to stop using the drug. These components all apply to cigarette smoking because of the presence of nicotine in tobacco.

The cigarette is a very efficient and well-designed system for administering nicotine. By inhaling, the smoker gets the drug to the brain very quickly. A typical smoker will take 10 puffs on a cigarette over a period of five minutes. In other words, people who smoke about one and a half packs (30 cigarettes) a day deliver 300 doses of nicotine to their brains daily.

Scientists studying addiction have observed that laboratory animals self-administer addictive substances. They accomplish this, for example, by pushing a lever to get repeated doses of a drug. Animals self-administer substances that are highly addictive in human beings, including morphine and cocaine. But they will not do this with nonaddictive substances.

The fact that animals self-administer addictive drugs like nicotine has changed the way researchers view addiction. Formerly, it was thought that addiction was a problem only for people with so-called addictive personalities. But it is now known that many addictive substances have similar chemical effects on the brain. In certain parts of the brain there is a chemical called dopamine, and this chemical is important to the functioning of human emotion and motivation. It is believed that addictive drugs affect the release of dopamine in the brain. So why do laboratory animals self-administer these drugs and humans become addicted to them? Because the release of dopamine in the brain results in a pleasant sense of well-being.

Nicotine artificially increases dopamine levels in the brain. This is the reward for the activity of smoking, and it causes a person to repeat the activities surrounding smoking. The process of being rewarded for an action is called reinforcement. Here is how the reinforcement process works: A person inhales the smoke from burning tobacco; this smoke contains the drug nicotine; the nicotine is absorbed into the blood through the lungs; in a few seconds the nicotine reaches the brain; the presence of nicotine leads to the release of dopamine; the dopamine produces a sense of well-being; this pleasant experience reinforces (that is, strengthens) the value of smoking tobacco while reducing concerns about the drawbacks of the activity. Thus, a person continues to smoke tobacco in order to deliver nicotine to the brain and experience the drug's pleasing effects. Because the effects of nicotine fade in a few minutes, the smoker must continue dosing (that is, smoking) frequently throughout the day to maintain the level of pleasure and prevent withdrawal. This is a simple explanation of how drugs such as nicotine that directly modify dopamine levels cause addictive behavior.

Researchers have developed ways to determine whether animals will self-administer a drug, which indicates that the drug is addictive. Then, to test the addictive properties of that drug, they observe whether the animals will stop using the drug if the release of dopamine is prevented during the drug's chemical reaction on the brain. Since the mid-1980s there has been clear evidence that laboratory animals will voluntarily self-administer nicotine and that these animals will reduce their self-administration if dopamine release in their brains is blocked.

Nicotine can work in the brain because the nicotine molecule is shaped like a neural transmitter called acetylcholine. Acetylcholine is a chemical found naturally in the nervous system that helps transmit information from one neuron to another. Also in the nervous system are receptors. These are specialized proteins that selectively bind drugs and initiate drug effects on the body. The receptors for acetylcholines are called cholinergic receptors. Nicotine acts on cholinergic receptors in the brain and other organs of the body. These receptors would normally be accepted by the body's own acetylcholine. But because nicotine activates cholinergic receptors, this heightens the release of other neurotransmitters and hormones. These include—in addition to acetylcholine—norepinephrine, dopamine, serotonin, and beta-endorphin.

What do these substances do for the user?

- Release of acetylcholine may improve work performance and memory.
- Increased release of norepinephrine, dopamine, and serotonin is associated with pleasure and appetite suppression.
- And the release of beta-endorphin may reduce anxiety and tension.

Scientific research is also beginning to show that nicotine may not be the only psychoactive ingredient in tobacco. Using advanced neuroimaging technology, scientists are finding in smokers a decreased level of monoamine oxidase (MAO), an important enzyme that is responsible for breaking down dopamine. The change in MAO must be caused by an ingredient in tobacco smoke other than nicotine because nicotine itself does not dramatically alter MAO levels. The decrease in MAO results in higher dopamine levels, which in turn bring on the desire for repeated use of the drug nicotine.

Exposure to nicotine causes the brain cells to compensate for the actions of the drug. This means that the cells must work to return the brain to its normal state of functioning. This process is called neuroadaptation. Neuroadaptation causes the brain to develop a tolerance for nicotine; that is, a given level of nicotine has less and less effect on the body. So higher levels of nicotine are needed to achieve the effects that lower doses formerly produced. When regular tobacco users spend a night sleeping, they regain some sensitivity to the effects of nicotine.

Once a user's brain has adapted so it can function normally in the presence of nicotine, it also becomes dependent on the presence of nicotine for such functioning. When nicotine is not available (as when a smoker stops smoking), brain function becomes disturbed, resulting in

MEASURING NICOTINE: GETTING MORE THAN YOU EXPECTED

Measuring the amount of nicotine in cigarettes is not as simple as one might imagine. The Massachusetts Department of Public Health (MDPH) developed a testing method using a machine that "smokes" the cigarettes tested. The machine simulates techniques used by smokers to increase the amount of drug inhaled. These include vent blocking, puffing more frequently, and inhaling more deeply, all factors that reflect average smoking practices. Massachusetts testing for nicotine yield produced numbers about twice as high as those found by the Federal Trade Commission (FTC). These numbers reveal that the average smoker receives much greater levels of nicotine than is suggested by FTC ratings.

People smoke cigarettes in various ways. So the MDPH tests produced a range of figures that describe the amount of nicotine—high, moderate, low, and nicotine free—delivered by a cigarette under average smoking conditions. This information allows smokers to compare nicotine levels among brands of cigarettes.

Of the 85 cigarette brands tested in 1997, 72 (85 percent) fell into the highest nicotine range, including many that are marketed as "light" cigarettes and even some marked as "ultra-light." Fifteen percent of cigarettes tested fell into the moderate range. Cigarettes with high and moderate yields can cause heavy dependence on nicotine.

The MDPH study shows that there are no significant differences in the total nicotine content of so-called full flavor, light, or ultra-light cigarettes. These terms mask the fact that all types of cigarettes are likely to contain similar amounts of nicotine in the unsmoked tobacco. People who think they can reduce their nicotine intake by smoking cigarettes advertised to be "lower yield" are mistaken.

FILTER VENTILATION

The amount of outside air allowed into the stream of smoke as it passes through the cigarette filter is regulated by the filter. There is a strong relationship between the percentage of filter ventilation and the type of cigarette. Full-flavor brands have filter ventilation of 0 to 25 percent. Light brands have filter ventilation ranging from 25 to 40 percent. And ultra-light cigarette brands have filter ventilation greater than 50 percent.

From these numbers one can see that it is the filter ventilation in cigarette design that defines "light" and "ultra-light," not the amount of nicotine in the cigarette itself. When outside air is allowed into the smoke stream as it passes through the filter, the contents of the smoke are diluted. But when smokers place their lips and fingers over the vents in the filter, they keep outside air from diluting the smoke, and so take in higher levels of tar and nicotine.

NICOTINE YIELD

Cigarettes do not deliver fixed amounts of tar and nicotine. How a person smokes a cigarette determines the amount of tar and nicotine that enters their body from the cigarette. The measure of the amount of nicotine in the smoke inhaled is called nicotine yield. This is not the amount of nicotine in cigarette tobacco; it is the amount of nicotine that actually finds its way into the body.

The MDPH testing method better simulates the behavior of the average smoker than does the FTC method. The MDPH method increases the amount of smoke inhaled with each puff of the smoking machine, reduces the amount of time taken between puffs, and requires that 50 percent of the cigarette filter be covered. The amount of nicotine that smokers inhale is based on the following factors:

- Puff volume, or how long and how deeply the smoke is inhaled
- Puff interval, or the amount of time between puffs
- The filter ventilation of the smoke inhaled, expressed as a percentage; the outside air that is drawn in through the filter tip mixes with the smoke and lessens its concentration

In 1994 the National Cancer Institute's Ad Hoc Committee of the President's Cancer Panel studied FTC testing for nicotine content in cigarettes. The committee reported that current FTC ratings provide little information for consumers who wish to know exactly how much nicotine they actually take in when smoking. In response to that report, the MDPH testing standards reflect current scientific knowledge about compensatory smoking and nicotine intake.

At a news conference in 1998, U.S. energy secretary Bill Richardson discussed a report on a European epilepsy drug that may help people quit smoking by blocking the effects of nicotine on the brain. Research into the chemistry of nicotine addiction may lead to more creative and effective ways of combating it.

a number of withdrawal symptoms, including restlessness, anxiety or tension, impatience, irritability or anger, difficulty concentrating, excessive hunger, depression, disorientation, loss of energy, dizziness, stomach or bowel problems, headache, sweating, difficulty with sleeping, heart palpitations, tremors, and, of course, a craving for more cigarettes.

Smokers use tobacco regularly because they are addicted to nicotine. However, most know tobacco is harmful and say they want to stop using it. Each year nearly 35 million smokers make a serious attempt to quit, but fewer than 7 percent of those who try to quit are successful for more than one year. Most relapse within a few days.

The inability to quit is not only a result of the addictiveness of nicotine. It is also because tobacco is easy and attractive to use and tobacco products are readily available. There are few legal and social consequences of tobacco use, and many sophisticated marketing and advertising methods encourage smoking. Combine these factors with nicotine's powerful addictive properties, and it is easy to understand why people who try tobacco ultimately become addicted to nicotine.

Although the exact nature of the link is unclear, research has shown that tobacco use is associated with both alcoholism and depression.

5

NICOTINE AND PSYCHOLOGICAL DISORDERS

A growing number of studies have linked smoking with poor mental health. Several of these have shown that patients with major depression are more likely to smoke than are members of the general population. These studies also reveal the influence of major depression on smoking cessation. A St. Louis survey, carried out in early 1980, contains information on both psychiatric diagnosis and smoking for more than 3,000 individuals. The survey confirms that major depression is more common among smokers than among nonsmokers (6.6 percent versus 2.9 percent) and that smokers with a lifetime history of major depression are less likely to succeed in quitting smoking than are smokers without such a history (14 percent versus 28 percent). The data also show that individuals with a lifetime history of depression are more likely to have smoked at any time in their lives (76 percent) than are those without such a history (52 percent).

Australian researchers found in 1998 that smokers have higher levels of anxiety, depression, alcohol abuse, and other psychological problems than nonsmokers. The findings also revealed that people with symptoms of depression were more than twice as likely to smoke than those without such symptoms.

Nicotine dependence is especially prevalent among alcohol and drug abusers. In fact, more than 80 percent of alcoholics are smokers, as are more than 50 percent of psychiatric patients.

SMOKING AND DEPRESSION

Today little information suggests that nicotine use directly causes depression. Most evidence indicates that it is nicotine withdrawal that provokes depression. A young adolescent with depressive symptoms would likely be tempted to use nicotine as a self-medication. This could explain why people who are depressed take up smoking at a higher rate than others. An alternative possibility is that regular nicotine use increases the likelihood of major depressive disorder. A third prospect is that some genetic trait independently increases the risk for both depression and smoking.

Medical literature strongly suggests that there is an association between cigarette smoking and both alcoholism and major depression. But, although smokers regularly report that nicotine diminishes anxiety, it has been difficult to prove this antianxiety effect of nicotine experimentally. Studies using laboratory animals fail to show a strong antianxiety effect for nicotine. However, nicotine dependence in these animals increases when they are under stress.

Regardless of the role of anxiety, there is little question that major depression is associated with cigarette smoking. The question is, what specifically is responsible for this? Are smoking and lifetime major depression associated because (1) one directly causes the other, (2) common social or environmental factors indirectly link them, or (3) the same genes increase the vulnerability to both conditions? Studies conclude that smoking does not cause depression, nor does depression cause smoking. The two are associated largely or entirely because of genetic factors that influence one's tendency toward both conditions.

It is important to recognize that the ability to see a link between smoking and major depression depends on social issues. If everyone smoked, there would be no association between smoking and any psychiatric illness. However, social pressures have ca sed community rates of smoking to fall. So individuals who can more easily quit do so. Those with greater vulnerability to nicotine are more likely to continue. As a result, as the social pressure to stop smoking grows, the association between smoking and depression becomes more apparent.

Do smokers with a previous experience of major depression develop depression during nicotine withdrawal? Studies of a group of placebo-treated smokers with a past history of depression show that 75 percent of the subjects reported developing depressed moods during the first week of withdrawal from nicotine, whereas 30 percent of smokers without such a history made a similar report. Thus, withdrawal was more severe in those smokers with a history of major depression. Their development of depression during the first week of withdrawal was associated with failure to succeed in giving up tobacco. A controlled study of smokers with histories of major depression has shown that they were much more successful in quitting smoking when given antidepressant medication in addition to health education.

More than 70 percent of persons diagnosed as schizophrenics smoke, compared with less than 30 percent of the general population. Smoking may improve a patient's mood or relieve the side effects of drugs, but given its enormous health risks, it cannot be seen as a real solution to emotional or mental problems.

Can cigarette smoking prevent or reduce the chances of depressive illness in some individuals? The answer to this intriguing question is not yet known. Most smokers with a history of depression fail when they try to stop smoking. It is not known if they would experience more than temporary depression if they were unable to resume smoking. More information is needed to determine if the long-term course of depression would be altered by the cessation of smoking. However, we live in an era in which a so-called smoke-free environment is considered desirable. Researchers have yet to investigate whether this societal pressure to stop smoking has unique risks for certain psychiatric patients.

There is a strong association between smoking and schizophrenia. According to a 1993 report by Alexander Glassman, 74 percent of a group of schizophrenic outpatients smoked. This contrasts sharply with the population as a whole—currently, under 30 percent of Americans smoke. Other studies of institutionalized schizophrenics have found that as many as 92 percent of the men and 82 percent of the women smoked. Clinical experience suggests that the heaviest smokers of all are found among institutionalized patients with chronic schizophrenia. Some researchers suggest that this high rate of cigarette smoking is an effort to reduce the unpleasant side effects that many schizophrenics experience from the drugs they take to control their ailment. But it is reasonable to wonder whether this very intense use of nicotine by chronic schizophrenic patients might not serve some more directly therapeutic purpose.

Epidemiologists—doctors who study the incidence of disease in populations—say that major depression is associated with a higher than average mortality rate. This is true even after accounting for suicide. But is this simply the expected mortality associated with a higher rate of smoking among depressed patients? This question has not been studied. As the number of smokers in America continues to diminish, an increasing percentage of those who remain smokers will be psychiatric patients. It is likely that some psychotropic drugs will help some of these troubled smokers give up tobacco.

However, not only is it more difficult for these individuals to quit smoking, but for some, successful cessation carries the risk of worsening their psychopathology. Understanding the basis of nicotine's association with schizophrenia and depression may open the way for new treatments of these devastating conditions.

An 8-year-old boy with attention deficit/hyperactivity disorder takes medication to help him master second-grade math. Some researchers have stated that smoking during pregnancy may cause future learning disabilities and behavioral problems in children due to fetal exposure to nicotine.

SMOKING AND ADHD

Some researchers think that smoking by women during pregnancy is an environmental factor associated with child behavioral problems such as attention deficit/hyperactivity disorder (ADHD). This is based on the belief that exposure to nicotine, the most potent psychoactive component of tobacco, damages the brain at critical times in the development of the fetus.

What is ADHD? Attention deficit/hyperactivity disorder is a chronic condition that begins in early childhood. It is manifested by a pattern of difficulties sustaining attention, excessive motor activity, and impulsive behavior. It is estimated that ADHD affects 6 to 9 percent of school-age children. Although there is no agreement regarding its cause, most investigators agree that the foundation of the disorder can be found in the patient's nervous system.

ADHD is thought to have both genetic and environmental causes. Studies of families, twins, and adopted children show that genetic factors appear to be an important part of the cause of ADHD. These same studies also provide solid evidence indicating that environmental factors are significant. Smoking by a woman during pregnancy, for example, is an environmental factor that may cause ADHD in her child.

An estimated 14.3 million women in the United States aged 18 to 44 are smokers. Since cigarette smoking is so common among women of childbearing age, information about the association between maternal smoking during pregnancy and ADHD in children could have a significant impact on public health.

Several animal studies of pregnant mice and rats show an association between the mother's chronic exposure to nicotine and hyperactive offspring. These studies illustrate the effect of nicotine on the developing fetus and demonstrate that exposure to nicotine results in tolerance to the drug.

Medical literature, too, suggests that maternal smoking is associated with behavioral difficulties in children. It is not clear whether this is specifically associated with ADHD. But it is known that nicotine can alter the activity of dopamine in the brain and that abnormal regulation of dopamine is believed to be involved in ADHD. So it is important to examine maternal smoking during pregnancy as a risk factor for ADHD in children.

An estimated 22 percent of mothers of ADHD children smoked during pregnancy. According to research findings, these mothers' tendency to smoke is not related to their IQ, to their socioeconomic status, or to whether or not they themselves have ADHD. Perhaps the mothers who smoke throughout pregnancy are not fully aware of the negative effects on their unborn children. Or perhaps they find it especially difficult to stop smoking for any length of time.

Other research indicates that smoking and ADHD may form a kind of vicious circle. Just as maternal smoking appears to contribute to ADHD, the disorder itself seems to increase the incidence of smoking.

As ADHD children reach adolescence, they are more likely to smoke than children who do not have the disorder. Furthermore, adult ADHD patients show higher rates of smoking than adults without ADHD.

Given all these factors, it appears that specific programs aimed at women of childbearing age—programs designed to convince them not to smoke or at least to stop smoking during pregnancy—could have a significant impact on public health.

In the public relations battle over smoking and its effects on health, any aspect of American culture may come under scrutiny. Robert Berliner, chairman of the board of the American Lung Association of Los Angeles, criticized the motion picture industry, including the movie Pulp Fiction, for glorifying tobacco use.

6

TREATMENT AND PREVENTION

How hard is it to quit smoking? The facts tell the story: only 33 percent of those who quit cigarettes without medical or other outside help (such as commercial cessation programs) remain free of tobacco for two days. Fewer than 5 percent of persons who try are ultimately successful at quitting. Why is nicotine dependence through cigarette smoking so strong? There are several reasons. Nicotine produces many positive effects that reinforce the smoking habit, including improved concentration and mood, decreased anger, and reduced weight. The nicotine reaches the brain just seconds after it is inhaled, producing an almost instantaneous effect. Furthermore, nicotine dosage can be precisely controlled by the way a cigarette is smoked, such as the depth of inhalation and how much of the tobacco is burned.

Symptoms of nicotine dependence and withdrawal can develop with all forms of tobacco use—cigarettes, chewing tobacco, snuff, pipes, and cigars. Withdrawal can be treated with nicotine replacements like nicotine gum, the nicotine patch, and nicotine nasal spray. The effectiveness of the treatment increases or decreases depending on how quickly the nicotine is absorbed, the size of the nicotine dose, and the availability of the product. These products all generate and maintain dependence, and if they are withheld withdrawal symptoms occur.

Smoking is the most important preventable cause of death and disease. Smoking is responsible for 20 percent of all deaths in the United States, and 45 percent of smokers will die of a tobacco-induced disorder. The most common smoking-related diseases and disorders are lung, oral, and other cancers; cardiovascular disease; chronic obstructive pulmonary disease; peptic ulcers; gastrointestinal disorders; and maternal or fetal complications. Secondhand (environmental) tobacco smoke causes the deaths of thousands of nonsmokers and weakens the health of children and other relatives of smokers. Smokeless tobacco, pipes, and cigars also cause oral cancers and other ailments.

Most tobacco-induced disorders appear to be caused by the carcinogens (cancer-causing agents) and carbon monoxide in tobacco smoke. If a nicotine-dependent person stops smoking, the risk of developing heart disease and cancer is dramatically reduced. Quitting also halts the deterioration in lung function of those with chronic obstructive lung disease.

NICOTINE WITHDRAWAL

What is it like to stop smoking? A person who has experienced nicotine withdrawal craves tobacco and desires sweet foods. Coughing sometimes increases, and the person's performance in tasks that require attentiveness and alertness may be impaired. Another less obvious effect of smoking cessation is a decline in the metabolic rate. Withdrawal symptoms begin a few hours after the last cigarette and peak within a day or two. Most symptoms last about four weeks, although heightened appetite and a craving for tobacco can last six months or more.

What causes these withdrawal symptoms? They are mainly the result of nicotine deprivation. It has been observed that withdrawal from cigarettes results in more discomfort than that caused by withdrawal from other forms of tobacco or from nicotine medications.

Withdrawal symptoms vary in severity depending on the individual. Cessation of smoking can produce clinically significant changes in the blood levels of several psychiatric medications. Withdrawal symptoms can also mimic, disguise, or aggravate the symptoms of other psychiatric disorders or the side effects of medications. For example, when an alcoholic who is also nicotine dependent is admitted to a smoke-free ward for alcohol detoxification, the anxiety, depression, difficulty concentrating, insomnia, irritability, and restlessness that he or she experiences could be due to or aggravated by nicotine withdrawal. Also, quitting smoking appears to cause a relapse of major depression, bipolar disorder, and alcohol and other drug problems.

For example, a random sample of 1,007 members of a large health maintenance organization in the Detroit area was interviewed in 1989. Members ranged in age from 21 to 30 years. Of that group, 394 persons acknowledged that they had smoked daily for at least one month in their lives; 241 (61.2 percent) of them reported that they had tried unsuccessfully at least once to quit or cut down on tobacco use. The variety of symptoms they reported are presented in the accompanying box.

THE REALITY OF WITHDRAWAL

Symptom	Number of Individuals	Percentage of Total
1. Craving for cigarettes	196	82.0
2. Irritability	147	61.5
3. Increased appetite	143	59.8
4. Restlessness	136	56.9
5. Nervousness	120	50.2
6. Trouble concentrating	65	27.2
7. Feeling depressed	54	22.6
8. Headache	43	18.0
9. Tremor	39	16.3
10. Drowsiness	31	13.0
11. Decreased heart rate	23	9.6
12. Upset stomach	21	8.8

BREAKING THE HABIT

It is often said that cigarette smoking is the single most important modifiable risk factor for illness and the greatest single cause of preventable premature deaths in the United States. What exactly can be expected when smokers "modify" their behavior? The evidence is clear that smoking cessation is effective in decreasing the risk of developing a host of tobacco-related illnesses. Fifteen years after giving up tobacco, the risk factor for coronary heart disease approaches that of individuals who never smoked. Within two years of quitting, the risk of having a heart attack decreases to a level similar to that for those who have never smoked.

Unfortunately, it is difficult to stop smoking, mainly because of the physical dependence on nicotine that plagues chronic smokers. But this dependence can now be treated effectively with a combination of behavioral and pharmacological methods. This combination roughly doubles the success rate over placebo treatments for individuals who are motivated to quit smoking. Smoking cessation can have an immediate positive impact on an individual's health; for example, a 35-year-old man who quits smoking will, on the average, increase his life expectancy by 5.1 years.

There are various ways to treat nicotine addiction, but the vast majority (95 percent) of people who stop using tobacco have received no formal help. They quit on their own. Some people are more likely to be successful at giving up their smoking habit than others. Factors that can influence the negative outcome of treatment include environmental stress; poor social support, such as being around family members who continue to smoke; lack of exposure to educational information; being

Women take a cigarette break outside their office building. With intolerance for smoking on the rise, many companies and building managers are implementing strict no-smoking policies, forcing smokers to stand outside the building.

female (yes, women have a tougher time quitting smoking than men); low self-confidence; and poor motivation.

Public information campaigns have been effective in reducing cigarette use, as has decreased tolerance in society and legislation. Joining self-help groups and seeing a physician can be beneficial. However, more intensive treatment programs may be necessary for individuals with high tobacco use, poor social adjustment, or other substance abuse problems.

Although it may seem unbelievable, the first pharmacological agent approved by the Food and Drug Administration (FDA) for use in smoking cessation therapy was nicotine. This is a case of the benefit of fighting fire with fire. Nicotine replacement therapies, such as nicotine gum, patches, nasal sprays, and inhalers, have been approved for use in the United States. They are all designed to relieve withdrawal symptoms. Using them produces less severe physiological alterations than tobacco-based systems, and they generally provide users with lower overall nicotine levels than tobacco. An added benefit is that these forms of nicotine have little abuse potential since they do not produce the pleasurable effects of tobacco products. Nor do they contain the carcinogens and gases associated with tobacco smoke.

The FDA's approval of nicotine gum in 1984 marked the availability (by prescription) of the first nicotine replacement therapy in the United States. In 1996 the FDA approved chewing gum containing nicotine for over-the-counter sales. Chewing nicotine gum interrupts smoking behavior while maintaining nicotine levels in the blood to minimize the effects of withdrawal. Three-month success rates of 76 percent and one-year success rates of 50 percent have been reported. This approach is most effective when it is accompanied by psychological therapy. Still, it has been found that there is considerable incidence of relapse after gum use is completed. While nicotine gum provides some smokers with control over dose and the ability to relieve cravings, others are unable to tolerate the taste or simply dislike chewing gum. In 1991 and 1992 the FDA approved four transdermal (allowing medication to be absorbed through the skin and into the bloodstream) nicotine patches, two of which became over-the-counter products in 1996. By transferring nicotine through the skin, these patches meet the needs of many tobacco users.

Data from the FDA and the pharmaceutical industry indicate that more than one million individuals have been successfully treated for

Nicorette gum and Zyban, a prescription drug, are two of the many products designed to help smokers suppress their cravings for nicotine. The number of such products has proliferated since the Food and Drug Administration approved the therapeutic use of nicotine in the mid-1980s.

nicotine addiction using nicotine gum or the transdermal patch. A nicotine nasal spray became available by prescription in 1996, and a nicotine inhaler was introduced in 1998. All of the nicotine replacement products appear to be equally effective. In fact, the combination of over-the-counter availability of these medications and intense media campaigns urging people to quit smoking have produced about a 20 percent increase in the number of people who successfully quit each year.

While doctors await the approval of a nicotine tablet that is dissolved under the tongue, researchers are voicing concern about the long-term physical effects of nicotine replacement therapies. Some smokers use nicotine replacement products for longer periods than is intended for these products. Now that these products have become readily available without a doctor's prescription, there is evidence of undesirable side effects from their long-term use.

Nicotine replacement products are also being considered as potential treatments for such chronic illnesses as Alzheimer's disease, Parkinson's disease, and Tourette's syndrome. But a 1998 study suggests that nicotine can damage cells that line blood vessels and the airways in the lungs. Researchers say that even though nicotine patches, gum, and other similar products are clearly safer than smoking, they should not be used for more than three to six months without medical supervision.

Nicotine is not the only substance used to relieve the symptoms of nicotine withdrawal. The first non-nicotine prescription drug, bupropion, an antidepressant marketed as Zyban, has been approved for use as a pharmacological treatment for nicotine addiction. Bupropion is the first drug designed to help people quit smoking that can be taken in pill form, and the first to contain no nicotine.

BEHAVIORAL TREATMENTS

Changing behavior can be integral in the treatment of nicotine addiction. This approach is found in clinic-based, formal smoking-cessation programs and in community and public health settings. It is even available over the telephone and in written formats as well. In general, behavioral methods are employed to (1) discover situations that increase the risk of relapse, (2) create a dislike of smoking, (3) develop a person's ability to self-monitor smoking behavior, and (4) establish ways to cope that compete with the addiction.

Other key factors in successful treatment include avoiding smokers and smoking environments and receiving support from family and

A woman lectures on the dangers of smoking. Smokers hoping to kick the habit may find strength in support groups and other social environments that reinforce their desire to quit.

friends. Most important, however, is learning and using the coping skills that prevent relapse. Smokers must learn behavioral and intellectual tools for relapse prevention, and they must be able to apply these skills in a crisis.

Behavioral and pharmacological treatments can be extremely successful when employed alone. But the integration of the two types of treatment is the most effective approach. More than 90 percent of the people who try to quit smoking either relapse or fully return to smoking within one year. The majority relapse within one week. However, an estimated 2.5 to 5 percent do succeed on their own. Pharmacological treatments can double these odds. A combination of pharmacological and behavioral treatments improves their chances even more. For example, when use of the nicotine patch is combined with a behavioral approach, such as group therapy or social support networks, the ability to quit smoking is significantly improved.

MOST TEEN SMOKERS BELIEVE THEY CAN QUIT BUT AFTER SIX YEARS 75% STILL SMOKE*

*it's not like they're addicted or anything.

CDC

The best treatment for nicotine dependence is prevention. Taking a lesson from the marketers of tobacco, the Centers for Disease Control and Prevention is aiming its message at teens.

Overall, intensive treatment produces good results. Intensive programs may apply successful treatment techniques from other substance abuse programs to the problem of nicotine addiction. These approaches include hypnosis, rapid smoking (aversive treatment), and nicotine blockade with the drug mecamylamine. The one-year postintervention effectiveness of most intensive smoking cessation programs is between

25 and 40 percent. This roughly parallels the postintervention effectiveness of programs for other forms of substance abuse.

THE BATTLE FOR PREVENTION

Smoking is clearly recognized as the most preventable cause of early death and disability. But only about 1 percent of the federal research budget is designated for medical research on the behavioral and psychiatric aspects of nicotine dependence. A number of health organizations have suggested programs for reducing the prevalence of tobacco use in our society. The American Psychiatric Association (APA), for example, has proposed a number of concrete policies and programs. These include (1) expanding teaching about the nature of nicotine dependence and its treatment in medical schools, psychiatric residency training programs, and continuing professional education programs to a level comparable to that for other substance-related disorders, (2) encouraging appropriate diagnosis and treatment of nicotine dependence as a condition related to other psychiatric disorders, (3) encouraging psychiatrists' role in the prevention of tobacco use because patients with other mental disorders are especially vulnerable to developing nicotine dependence, (4) supporting the development of smoke-free policies in all health care facilities and in society at large, and (5) advocating health insurance coverage for the treatment of nicotine dependence by qualified health professionals. The APA has endorsed policies designed to help prevent and reduce smoking, including the following:

- Prohibiting advertising and sports-activity sponsorships that promote tobacco use.
- Controlling the availability of tobacco products to young persons by establishing a national minimum age of 21 years for the purchase of tobacco products.
- Banning the sale of tobacco products through vending machines.
- Enforcing existing laws regulating the sale of tobacco products.
- Eliminating subsidies and all other forms of governmental assistance that encourage the production or export of tobacco and tobacco products.
- Encouraging funding of transition programs to help those with tobacco-related jobs find new employment.
- Increasing state and federal taxes on tobacco products and

applying the proceeds of such taxes to the prevention, treatment, and research of nicotine dependence.

- Rewording the warning labels on tobacco products to include the likelihood of the user's developing dependence on nicotine.

The American Psychiatric Association encourages early efforts in the public schools to inform young people about the high risk of developing nicotine dependence after experimenting with tobacco and about the health hazards that go along with being dependent on the drug. The association also suggests that public health efforts should be expanded to counter the seductive message of tobacco advertising.

In coming years, as states develop antismoking programs with funds provided by the 1998 tobacco-industry settlement, many of the American Psychiatric Association's proposals will likely be adopted. Already many billboards are displaying antismoking messages rather than cigarette ads, and prohibitions against selling tobacco products to young people are being more strictly enforced. Yet the tobacco industry continues to exert a strong influence on public policy at both the state and the federal level. The campaign against the harmful effects of tobacco is still in its early stages.

APPENDIX

FOR MORE INFORMATION

Action on Smoking and Health
2013 H Street NW
Washington, DC 20006
202-659-4310
http://www.ash.org

American Cancer Society
1599 Clifton Road NE
Atlanta, GA 30329
800-227-2345
http://www.cancer.org

American Heart Association
7272 Greenville Avenue
Dallas, TX 75231
214-373-6300
http://www.americanheart.org

American Lung Association
1740 Broadway
New York, NY 10019
800-LUNG-USA
http://www.lungusa.org/tobacco

American Psychiatric Association
1400 K Street NW
Washington, DC 20005
202-682-6000
E-mail: apa@psych.org
http://www.psych.org

Centers for Disease Control and Prevention
1600 Clifton Road, NE
Atlanta, GA 30333
http://www.cdc.gov/nccdphp/osh/

Environmental Protection Agency
401 M Street
Washington, DC 20460-0003
202-260-2090
http://www.epa.gov

Food and Drug Administration
5600 Fishers Lane
Rockville, MD 20857
888-INFO-FDA
http://www.fda.gov

National Cancer Institute
Cancer Information Service
800-4-CANCER
TTY: 800-332-8615
http://cancernet.nci.nih.gov

National Center for Tobacco-Free Kids
800-284-KIDS
http://www.tobaccofreekids.org

National Clearinghouse on Alcohol and Drug Information
P.O. Box 2345
Rockville, MD 20847-2345
800-729-6686
TDD: 800-487-4899
http://www.health.org

Stop Teenage Addiction to Tobacco (STAT)
Northeastern University
360 Huntington Ave.
241 Cushing Hall
Boston, MA 02115
617-373-7828
http://www.stat.org

Tobacco BBS
http://www.tobacco.org
212-982-4645

Percentage of High School Students Who Currently Use Cigarettes, Smokeless Tobacco, or Cigars, by Gender, Race/Ethnicity, and Grade

Category	Cigarettes (%)	Smokeless Tobacco (%)	Cigars (%)
Gender			
Male	37.7	15.8	31.2
Female	34.7	1.5	10.8
Race/Ethnicity			
White, non-Hispanic	39.7	12.2	22.5
Male	39.6	20.6	32.5
Female	39.9	1.6	9.6
Black, non-Hispanic	22.7	2.2	19.4
Male	28.2	3.2	28.1
Female	17.4	1.3	11.0
Hispanic	34.0	5.1	20.3
Male	35.5	8.4	26.3
Female	32.3	1.2	13.0
Grade			
9	33.4	9.7	17.3
10	35.3	6.8	22.3
11	36.6	10.0	24.2
12	39.6	10.5	23.8
Total % Surveyed	36.4	9.3	22.0

Source: Centers for Disease Control and Prevention, "Tobacco Use Among High School Students—United States, 1997," *Morbidity and Mortality Weekly Report* 47, no. 12 (1998): 229–233.

APPENDIX

ANNUAL CIGARETTE CONSUMPTION AMONG ADULTS

Total and Per Capita Manufactured Cigarette Consumption and Percentage Change in Per Capita Consumption in the United States from 1900 to 1995

Year	Total (Billion)	Per Capita (17 years or older)	Percentage Change in Per Capita Consumption from Previous Year
1900	2.5	54	
1901	2.5	53	− 1.9
1902	2.8	60	+ 13.2
1903	3.1	64	+ 6.7
1904	3.3	66	+ 3.1
1905	3.6	70	+ 6.1
1906	4.5	86	+ 22.9
1907	5.3	99	+ 15.1
1908	5.7	105	+ 6.1
1909	7.0	125	+ 19.0
1910	8.6	151	+ 20.8
1911	10.1	173	+ 14.6
1912	13.2	223	+ 28.9
1913	15.8	260	+ 16.6
1914	16.5	267	+ 2.7
1915	17.9	285	+ 6.7
1916	25.2	395	+ 38.6
1917	35.7	551	+ 39.5
1918	45.6	697	+ 26.5
1919	48.0	727	+ 4.3
1920	44.6	665	− 8.5
1921	50.7	742	+ 11.6
1922	53.4	770	+ 3.8
1923	64.4	911	+ 18.3
1924	71.0	982	+ 7.8
1925	79.8	1,085	+ 10.5
1926	89.1	1,191	+ 9.8
1927	97.5	1,279	+ 7.4

Year	Total (Billion)	Per Capita (17 years or older)	Percentage Change in Per Capita Consumption from Previous Year
1928	106.0	1,366	+ 6.8
1929	118.6	1,504	+ 10.1
1930	119.3	1,485	− 1.3
1931	114.0	1,399	− 5.8
1932	102.8	1,245	− 11.0
1933	111.6	1,334	+ 7.1
1934	125.7	1,483	+ 11.2
1935	134.4	1,564	+ 5.5
1936	152.7	1,754	+ 12.1
1937	162.8	1,847	+ 5.3
1938	163.4	1,830	− 0.9
1939	172.1	1,900	+ 3.8
1940	181.9	1,976	+ 4.0
1941	208.9	2,236	+ 13.2
1942	245.0	2,585	+ 15.6
1943	284.3	2,956	+ 14.4
1944	296.3	3,039	+ 2.8
1945	340.6	3,449	+ 13.5
1946	344.3	3,446	− 0.1
1947	345.4	3,416	− 0.9
1948	358.9	3,505	+ 2.6
1949	360.9	3,480	− 0.7
1950	369.8	3,552	+ 2.1
1951	397.1	3,744	+ 5.4
1952	416.0	3,886	+ 3.8
1953	408.2	3,778	− 2.8
1954	387.0	3,546	− 6.1
1955	396.4	3,597	+ 1.4
1956	406.5	3,650	+ 1.5
1957	422.5	3,755	+ 2.9
1958	448.9	3,953	+ 5.3
1959	467.5	4,073	+ 3.0
1960	484.4	4,171	+ 2.4
1961	502.5	4,266	+ 2.3
1962	508.4	4,266	0.0
1963	523.9	4,345	+ 1.9
1964	511.3	4,194	− 3.5
1965	528.8	4,258	+ 1.5
1966	541.3	4,287	+ 0.7
1967	549.3	4,280	− 0.2

Year	Total (Billion)	Per Capita (17 years or older)	Percentage Change in Per Capita Consumption from Previous Year
1968	545.6	4,186	− 2.2
1969	528.9	3,993	− 4.6
1970	536.5	3,985	− 0.2
1971	555.1	4,037	+ 1.3
1972	566.8	4,043	+ 0.1
1973	589.7	4,148	+ 2.6
1974	599.0	4,141	− 0.2
1975	607.2	4,122	− 0.5
1976	613.5	4,091	− 0.8
1977	617.0	4,043	− 1.2
1978	616.0	3,970	− 1.8
1979	621.5	3,861	− 2.7
1980	631.5	3,849	− 0.3
1981	640.0	3,836	− 0.3
1982	634.0	3,739	− 2.5
1983	600.0	3,488	− 6.7
1984	600.4	3,446	− 1.2
1985	594.0	3,370	− 2.2
1986	583.8	3,274	− 2.8
1987	575.0	3,197	− 2.4
1988	562.5	3,096	− 3.3
1989	540.0	2,926	− 5.5
1990	525.0	2,826	− 3.4
1991	510.0	2,720	− 3.8
1992	500.0	2,641	− 2.9
1993	485.0	2,538	− 3.9
1994	485.0	2,522	− 0.6
1995 (est.)	487.0	2,515	− 0.3

Source: Tobacco Information and Prevention Source (TIPS), "Consumption Data," Atlanta: Office on Smoking and Health, National Center for Chronic Disease Prevention and Health Promotion, Centers for Disease Control and Prevention. http://www.cdc.gov/nccdphp/osh/consump1.htm.

APPENDIX

BIBLIOGRAPHY

American Cancer Society. *Cancer Facts and Figures: 1996.* Atlanta: American Cancer Society, 1996.

American Psychiatric Association. *Diagnostic and Statistical Manual of Mental Disorders*, 4th ed. Washington, D.C.: American Psychiatric Press, 1994.

Centers for Disease Control and Prevention. "Cigarette Smoking Among Adults: United States, 1994." *Morbidity and Mortality Weekly Report* 45, no. 27 (1996): 588–590.

———. "Tobacco Use Among High School Students—United States, 1997." *Morbidity and Mortality Weekly Report* 47, no. 12 (1998): 229–233.

———. "Mortality Trends for Selected Smoking-Related and Breast Cancer—United States, 1950–1990." *Morbidity and Mortality Weekly Report* 42, no. 44 (1993): 857, 863–866.

———. "Smoking-Attributable Mortality and Years of Potential Life Lost—United States, 1990." *Morbidity and Mortality Weekly Report* 42, no. 33 (1993): 645–648.

Environmental Protection Agency. *Respiratory Health Effects of Passive Smoking: Lung Cancer and Other Disorders.* Washington, D.C.: U.S. Environmental Protection Agency, Office of Health and Environmental Assessment, Office of Research and Development. EPA/600/6–90/006F. December 1992.

Glassman, A. H. "Cigarette Smoking: Implications for Psychiatric Illness." *American Journal of Psychiatry* 150, no. 4 (1993).

The Health Consequences of Smoking: A Public Health Service Review. Washington, D.C.: U.S. Government Printing Office, 1967.

U. S. Department of Agriculture. *Tobacco Situation and Outlook Report.* Washington, D.C.: U. S. Government Printing Office, September 1987, April 1996.

U. S. Surgeon General's Advisory Committee on Smoking and Health. *Smoking and Health: Report of the Advisory Committee to the Surgeon General of the Public Health Service.* Washington, D.C.: U.S. Government Printing Office, 1964.

American Cancer Society. *Cancer Facts and Figures—1998*. Atlanta: American Cancer Society, 1998.

American Psychiatric Association. *Diagnostic and Statistical Manual of Mental Disorders*, 4th ed. Washington, D.C.: American Psychiatric Press, 1994.

Bartecchi, C. E., T. D. MacKenzie, and R. W. Schrier. "Human Costs of Tobacco Use." *New England Journal of Medicine* 330 (1994): 907–980.

Centers for Disease Control and Prevention. *Preventing Tobacco Use Among Young People: A Report of the Surgeon General*. Washington, D.C.: U.S. Department of Health and Human Services, 1994.

Department of Health and Human Services. *The Health Benefits of Smoking Cessation*. Rockville, Md.: U.S. Department of Health and Human Services, Public Health Service, Centers for Disease Control and Prevention, Center for Chronic Disease Prevention and Health Promotion, Office on Smoking and Health. DHHS publication no. (CDC) 90–8416, 1990.

Glantz, Stanton A., et al. *The Cigarette Papers*. San Francisco: University of California Press, 1996.

Henningfield, J. E. "Nicotine Medications for Smoking Cessation." *New England Journal of Medicine* 333 (1995): 1196–1203.

Henningfield, Jack. *Nicotine: An Old-Fashioned Addiction*. New York: Chelsea House, 1992.

Kluger, Richard. *Ashes to Ashes: America's Hundred-Year Cigarette War, the Public Health, and the Unabashed Triumph of Philip Morris*. New York: Alfred A. Knopf, 1996.

Krogh, David. Smoking: *The Artificial Passion*. New York: W. H. Freeman, 1991.

Lynch, Barbara S., and Richard J. Bonnie. *Growing Up Tobacco Free*. Washington, D.C.: National Academy Press, 1994.

Martin, W. R., G. R. Van Loon, E. T. Iwamoto, and L. Davis, eds. *Tobacco Smoking and Nicotine.* New York: Plenum Publishing, 1987.

Paper, Jordan. *Offering Smoke: The Sacred Pipe and Native American Religion.* Moscow, Idaho: University of Idaho Press, 1988.

Stronck, David R. *Tobacco: The Real Story.* Santa Cruz, Calif.: Network Publications, 1987.

APPENDIX

GLOSSARY

Addiction: A chronic disease characterized by compulsive desire for or dependence on a habit-forming substance, usually of a harmful nature (such as nicotine, alcohol, heroin, or cocaine). Addiction typically results in the development of tolerance and craving.

Asthma: A respiratory condition that results in episodes of difficulty with breathing.

Cancer: A disorder in which body cells begin to divide uncontrollably, producing tumors that enlarge and can spread to adjacent tissues.

Carbon monoxide: An odorless, potentially toxic gas that is created when fuel is burned. Cigarette smoke contains carbon monoxide.

Carcinogen: A substance or other factor (such as radiation) that causes cancer.

Cessation: Stopping or ceasing some activity either forever or for some time.

Cigar: Coarsely shredded tobacco that is rolled in a thick, dark paper or tobacco leaf and smoked.

Cigarette: Finely shredded tobacco that is rolled in thin paper and smoked.

Compensation: Behavior patterns in which the smoker makes up for low levels of nicotine yield by increasing the amount of nicotine taken from the cigarette. Typical patterns of compensation include smoking more often, smoking more cigarettes on a given occasion, smoking more deeply, and increasing the puff volume or length of time smoke is inhaled.

Craving: A powerful, often uncontrollable desire for drugs.

Dip: Moist snuff, a smokeless tobacco.

Dopamine: A neurotransmitter present in regions of the brain that regulates movement, emotion, motivation, and the feeling of pleasure.

Dose: The amount of a medicine or drug to be taken at one time.

Emphysema: A lung disease in which tissue deterioration results in increased air retention and reduced exchange of gases. The result is difficulty in breathing and shortness of breath. The disease is often caused by smoking.

Environmental smoke: See **Secondhand smoke**.

Malignant tumor: A dangerous, virulent cancerous growth in the body that may cause death; usually caused by a carcinogen.

Moist snuff: A smokeless tobacco product containing powdered tobacco and a wetting agent.

Neurotransmitter: A natural substance that transmits nerve impulses or signals. Nicotine stimulates the release of neurotransmitters that can affect heart rate, blood pressure, and moods.

Nicotine: A toxic, addictive substance contained in tobacco. In the tobacco plant, nicotine helps defend against insects.

Nicotine content: The amount of nicotine contained in the tobacco of a cigarette or other product before it is burned and inhaled. The nicotine is released into the smoke when the tobacco is burned, and the smoker extracts it by inhaling.

Nicotine yield: The amount of nicotine present in the smoke that is drawn from a cigarette or other tobacco product.

Physical dependence: A condition that occurs with regular drug use and results in withdrawal syndrome when drug use is stopped; usually occurs once tolerance has been established.

Placebo: A harmless, unmedicated preparation given as a medicine to a patient as a control in testing the effects of another, medicated substance.

Psychoactive: Having a specific effect on the mind, such as that produced by using a drug or chemical.

Rush: A surge of pleasure that rapidly follows the administration of some drugs, such as nicotine.

Secondhand smoke: Also known as environmental smoke or environmental tobacco smoke (ETS), it is the smoke that escapes from a burning cigarette, cigar, or pipe into the surrounding air, or the smoke that a smoker blows out after inhaling. Secondhand smoke is a potential health hazard to those who never smoke.

Snuff: A smokeless tobacco product containing powdered tobacco.

Substance: A drug of abuse, a medication, or a toxin.

Tar: Small particles produced by burning tobacco. When inhaled with tobacco smoke, these can cause cancer and damage lungs.

Tobacco: A plant widely cultivated for its leaves, which are used primarily for smoking; the *tabacum* species is the major source of tobacco products.

Tolerance: A condition in which higher doses of a drug are required to produce the same effect as that experience during initial use; often leads to physical dependence.

Withdrawal: A variety of symptoms that occur after use of an addictive drug is reduced or stopped.

APPENDIX

INDEX

APPENDIX

PICTURE CREDITS

Senior Consulting Editor Carol C. Nadelson, M.D., is president and chief executive officer of the American Psychiatric Press, Inc., staff physician at Cambridge Hospital, and clinical professor of psychiatry at Harvard Medical School. In addition to her work with the American Psychiatric Association, which she served as vice president in 1981–83 and president in 1985–86, Dr. Nadelson has been actively involved in other major psychiatric organizations, including the Group for the Advancement of Psychiatry, the American College of Psychiatrists, the Association for Academic Psychiatry, the American Association of Directors of Psychiatric Residency Training Programs, the American Psychosomatic Society, and the American College of Mental Health Administrators. In addition, she has been a consultant to the Psychiatric Education Branch of the National Institute of Mental Health and has served on the editorial boards of several journals. Doctor Nadelson has received many awards, including the Gold Medal Award for significant and ongoing contributions in the field of psychiatry, the Elizabeth Blackwell Award for contributions to the causes of women in medicine, and the Distinguished Service Award from the American College of Psychiatrists for outstanding achievements and leadership in the field of psychiatry.

Consulting Editor Claire E. Reinburg, M.A., is editorial director of the American Psychiatric Press, Inc., which publishes about 60 new books and six journals a year. She is a graduate of Georgetown University in Washington, D.C., where she earned bachelor of arts and master of arts degrees in English. She is a member of the Council of Biology Editors, the Women's National Book Association, the Society for Scholarly Publishing, and Washington Book Publishers.

Daniel Partner is an author who lives and works in northern Vermont. His recent books include *The One Year Book of Poetry* and *Women of Sacred Song: Meditations on Hymns by Women.*